REINER SCHÜRMANN AND THE POETICS OF POLITICS

Before you start to read this book, take this moment to think about making a donation to punctum books, an independent non-profit press,

@ https://punctumbooks.com/support/

If you're reading the e-book, you can click on the image below to go directly to our donations site. Any amount, no matter the size, is appreciated and will help us to keep our ship of fools afloat. Contributions from dedicated readers will also help us to keep our commons open and to cultivate new work that can't find a welcoming port elsewhere. Our adventure is not possible without your support.
Vive la open-access.

Fig. 1. Hieronymus Bosch, *Ship of Fools* (1490–1500)

REINER SCHÜRMANN AND THE POETICS OF POLITICS. Copyright © 2018 by Christopher P. Long. This work carries a Creative Commons BY-NC-SA 4.0 International license, which means that you are free to copy and redistribute the material in any medium or format, and you may also remix, transform and build upon the material, as long as you clearly attribute the work to the authors (but not in a way that suggests the authors or punctum books endorses you and your work), you do not use this work for commercial gain in any form whatsoever, and that for any remixing and transformation, you distribute your rebuild under the same license. http://creativecommons.org/licenses/by-nc-sa/4.0/

First published in 2018 by dead letter office, BABEL Working Group
an imprint of punctum books, Earth, Milky Way.
https://punctumbooks.com

The BABEL Working Group is a collective and desiring-assemblage of scholar-gypsies with no leaders or followers, no top and no bottom, and only a middle. BABEL roams and stalks the ruins of the post-historical university as a multiplicity, a pack, looking for other roaming packs with which to cohabit and build temporary shelters for intellectual vagabonds. We also take in strays.

ISBN-13: 978-1-947447-73-8 (print)
ISBN-13: 978-1-947447-74-5 (ePDF)

LCCN: 2018948913
Library of Congress Cataloging Data is available from the Library of Congress

Book design: Vincent W.J. van Gerven Oei
Cover image: Louis Comtois, "Riddle of the Sphinx: In the Morning on Four, at Noon on Two, in the Evening on Three," 1989. Oil, wax, mixed media on plywood. 203.2 × 595.4 cm. Purchase, with generous funds from the artist and Reiner Schürmann, with the collaboration of the American Friends of Canada © Musée d'art contemporain de Montréal. Photo: Richard-Max Tremblay.

Reproduction on page 59 of Reiner Schürmann's article "Situating René Char: Hölderlin, Heidegger, Char and the 'There Is,'" *boundary 2* 4, no. 2 (1976): 513–34, 514, containing Henri Matisse's drawing "The Shark and the Gull," first published in *Cahiers d'Art* 1945–46, with kind permission of *Cahiers d'Art*.

HIC SVNT MONSTRA

Christopher P. Long

Reiner Schürmann
and the Poetics of Politics

Contents

¶ *Introduction* · Awakening to Symbols · 15   ¶ *Morning* · The Duplicity of Beginning · 37   ¶ *Afternoon* · Situating the Poetics of Politics · 63   ¶ *Evening* · The Voice of Singularity and a Philosophy to Come · 105   ¶ A Politics of the Between · 135 ¶ Bibliography · 161

For Reiner Schürmann

Acknowledgments

If my encounters with Reiner Schürmann during the final two years of his life taught me the power of beginning even in the shadow of death, my life with Valerie over the last twenty years, and with Chloe and Hannah since they were born, has taught me the meaning of happiness in its deepest, most ancient sense. They remind me that a life well-lived unfolds each day as we commit our best selves to one another in the rhythm of our finite lives. This book could not have been born without their love and support which makes my life not only possible, but infinitely richer and more beautiful.

To write a book that uncovers the hegemonic operation of principles in setting the world in order while serving as Dean of the College of Arts & Letters at Michigan State University might seem at first incongruent. Indeed, this book was first conceived while I was a junior member of the faculty at the Richard Stockton College of New Jersey, and two of the three chapters that make it a tryptic were developed while I was a faculty member and Associate Dean at the Pennsylvania State University. Yet the path that has led me to administration has also been shaped by the teaching of Reiner Schürmann. Whatever else an administrative life involves, at its heart it ought to be animated by the meaning of its Latin root, *ministrare,* "to serve, attend, wait upon." The attentive service of administration should always remain attuned to the manner in which principles shape and misshape our relationships with one another over the course of our academic lives conditioned as they are by natality and mortality. The institutions that have supported and sustained my academic and administrative work have sought to embody the public educational mission that motivated their creation. Founded in 1969, The Richard Stockton College of New Jersey was established to develop engaged citizens in a rapidly changing interdependent world. A century earlier, a similar vision led to the creation of Michigan State University and, ten days later, The Pennsylvania State University as the pioneering land-grant institutions embodying the Morrill Act's commitment to "promote the liberal and practical education of the industrial classes in the several pursuits and professions in life."* If these institutions embody the traits of natality Schürmann often associates with principles of domination and hegemony, they also open spaces of educational encounter capable of transforming lives by cultivating habits of critical thinking and acting attuned the conditions of finitude that shape our relationships with one another.

This book owes its existence also to these institutions, and to the Graduate Faculty at the New School for Social Research, which opened a space for just such an encounter with the remarkable teacher to whom this book is dedicated.

Finally, this book is published and made accessible to the public by punctum books under the visionary leadership of Eileen Joy and Vincent W.J. van Gerven Oei. I would like to thank them both for their tireless efforts to bring this text to publication, and for their steadfast commitment to the practice of making ideas public so they might shape more just and beautiful futures.

---

* Act of July 2, 1862 (Morrill Act), Public Law 37-108, which established land grant colleges, 07/02/1862; Enrolled Acts and Resolutions of Congress, 1789-1996; Record Group 11; General Records of the United States Government; National Archives.

Introduction
Awakening to Symbols

*To think is to pause and dwell on the
conditions of what one is living.*

— Reiner Schürmann[1]

To begin with a thinker who remained always attuned to the duplicitous nature of beginning requires candor. There is a thetic dimension to every beginning, and we will do well not to deny it here. Rather, let us begin by attending to the things Reiner Schürmann himself said about beginning: "A starting point," he wrote, "that neither abandons ordinary experience nor transsubstantiates it into the extra-ordinary will have to be looked for in something everyone is familiar with, however poorly ...."[2] For Schürmann, the ultimate traits of everydayness with which we are all familiar, though poorly, are the irreducible phenomena of natality and mortality that condition our human existence.

But perhaps in pointing already at the outset to these ultimate conditions, we have stepped back behind ordinary experience too quickly. Perhaps we ought to return to an experience

---

[1] Reiner Schürmann, "Abstraction That Makes the Viewer Think About the Last Paintings of Louis Comtois," *C Magazine* 29 (1991): 6–7.
[2] Reiner Schürmann, "Conditions of Evil," in *Deconstruction and the Possibility of Justice*, eds. Drucilla Cornell, Michel Rosenfeld, and David Gray Carlson (New York: Routledge, 1992), 388.

of a beginning, to the place and time of my first real encounter with Reiner Schürmann, to a memory dimly recalled, yet poignant and delightful — like the man himself.

Early in the fall semester of 1991, my first as a graduate student at the Graduate Faculty of the New School for Social Research, a group of us found ourselves closely packed into a rather large room in the Cardozo School of Law. We had come to hear Jacques Derrida, who was to speak on a panel organized by Drucilla Cornell for a conference entitled, "The Politics of Transformation and the Limit of the Imagination." But what I remember most clearly from that day was Reiner Schürmann.

The content of the paper he delivered was largely lost on me; as a new graduate student in the heady intellectual world of New York City, I was barely treading water. Years later, quite recently in fact, I came to realize that the paper Schürmann presented entitled, "Conditions of Evil," had been adapted from what was to become the final chapter of his magnum opus, *Broken Hegemonies*.

We will return to that paper and to the final chapter of *Broken Hegemonies* in a moment, for it too has something to teach us about beginnings.

What struck me then, however, and what has remained with me since, is a single sentence Schürmann uttered that day, and the embodied gesture that went with it. It has stayed with me in part, I imagine, because it became a story to which my graduate student colleagues and I returned with delight and perplexity in the months and years that followed.

What prompted Schürmann's response, my friend and graduate school colleague, Emma Bianchi, has recently reminded me, was the way Derrida and Cornell made use of the idea of sexual difference.[3] Now Reiner was an elegant man: tall and

---

3 Emma's own work engages the questions of embodiment, gender, and sexuality in Schürmann in generative and insightful ways, despite the fact, as she herself recognizes and as we will hear presently, that Schürmann rejected "sexual difference as a relevant category of philosophical analysis and his utter silence on matters of sexuality more generally." See Emanuela Bianchi, "Natal Bodies, Mortal Bodies, Sexual Bodies: Reading Gender, Desire, and

poised and daunting. But he also had a playful sense of humor, childlike in the deepest philosophical sense. And when he was in the throes of debate or found himself intent on emphasizing a point of significance, his voice would deepen slightly and take on a dimension of exasperation; the pace of his words would quicken and become more enunciated. If he was wearing his reading glasses at the time, he would push them slightly down on his nose, looking over them directly at the person with whom he was speaking. If you were lucky, that look came with an impish smile, the sign of a playfulness that meant something significant was at stake. If you were not, that look was sharp and serious, the sign that you had gone down a disappointing track. This later was the look we students came to fear; but more often than not in public discussions with colleagues, it was the former, more playful look Schürmann gave.

That was the look that captured our attention that early fall day in 1991; but what perplexed and delighted us was what he said to Derrida and Cornell over the rim of his glasses: "I find that metaphysical and very, very boring." The way he slowed his speech down and elongated the "o" in "boring" to emphasize the words "very, very bo-o-oring," was something we continue to mimic even today when we are together. And, of course, thereafter too we started playfully accusing one another of "being metaphysical" and therefore "very, very bo-o-oring" whenever we had an opportunity to disagree.

At the time, however, I had no idea what it could mean to be metaphysical, let alone why it was so "very, very boring." But I did know one thing: I wanted to learn what Reiner Schürmann had to teach.

The Tragic Situation

Although it was by no means clear to me at the time, the paper Schürmann delivered at the conference contained one of the

---

Kinship through Reiner Schürmann's *Broken Hegemonies*," *Graduate Faculty Philosophy Journal* 33, no. 1 (April 1, 2012): 57–84, at 57.

central lessons of his teaching. This lesson has less to do with the metaphysics Schürmann found so very boring than it does with learning how to respond to the tragic conditions under which human life unfolds. The response to which he gestures in the paper he delivered that day is more fully fleshed out in *Broken Hegemonies*, a text that undertakes what Schürmann calls a "phenomenology of ultimates" that attempts "to grasp irreducible traits in everydayness and put them to the test of a historical-systematic investigation."[4] The historical investigation we find in *Broken Hegemonies* traces the trajectory of the sort of metaphysical thinking Schürmann found so exasperatingly boring that September day in 1991. It uncovers over the course of 600 pages the way in which the ultimate principles that set an epoch into order win legitimacy and authority only by denying the thetic act that posits them as normatively binding in the first place. Metaphysical beginnings, for Schürmann, are duplicitous precisely because they cover over their own thetic origin in the hopes of winning legitimacy. They become, to adopt Schürmann's language, enamored with their own hegemonic fantasms. Such metaphysical principles are hegemonic, because they reign with authority; they are fantastic, because they depend ultimately upon the delusion of immaculate birth that requires the denial of the very thetic act that enables them, for a time, to reign supreme.

This denial always comes back to haunt the epoch it establishes. The story of *Broken Hegemonies* is the history of metaphysical principles as they are posited, reign, and wither under the weight of their own delusion. To philosophy Schürmann assigns the "task of showing the tragic condition beneath all principled constructions."[5] Nowhere is the tragic force of hegemonic principles in conflict with one another more poignantly illustrated than in the ancient Greek tragedies of Sophocles and Aeschylus. Agamemnon's rejection of his paternal responsibilities

---

4 Schürmann, "Conditions of Evil," 388–89.
5 Reiner Schürmann, *Broken Hegemonies*, trans. Reginald Lilly (Bloomington: Indiana University Press, 2003), 3.

at Aulus by sacrificing his daughter, Iphigeneia, in order to enable the Greeks to prosecute the war at Troy is, for Schürmann, the paradigmatic instance of tragic denial in the face of conflicting principles.[6] But at the beginning of *Broken Hegemonies*, it is Antigone who embodies the tragic double bind that conditions all principled constructions. Schürmann begins with Antigone, for her situation demonstrates more clearly than Agamemnon's how the conflict of principles singularize: "Antigone ends up broken, not exactly by disparate laws but—as we shall see—*singularized under one law, through a withdrawal toward the other.*"[7] This way of formulating the tragic situation points already to the ultimate conditions under which principles are always deployed, to the traits of natality and mortality with which we are all familiar however poorly. Schürmann begins with Antigone because she is so poignantly singularized by the interplay of natality and mortality in the *Antigone*. When she refuses, at the beginning, to remain silent about her intentions to bury her brother, Polyneices, despite her sister's entreaties, she embodies the trait of natality that "prompts us toward new commencings and sovereign commandings. It makes us magnify standards."[8] When she is sent, suffering, underground, she embodies the trait of mortality that "always pulls us back from the world of such archic referents. It is a singularizing, dispersing, desolating, evicting, dephenomenolizing, exclusory trait."[9] In sending her to a cave underground, Sophocles has Creon speak the language of marriage as he insists upon "enfolding her in her rocky

---

6 See, for example, ibid., 26–28, 621–22. For a detailed discussion of the tragic dynamics Agamemnon faced at Aulus, see Christopher P. Long, "The Daughters of Metis: Patriarchal Dominion and the Politics of the Between," *The Graduate Faculty Philosophy Journal* 28, no. 2 (2007): 67–86.
7 Schürmann, *Broken Hegemonies*, 3–4.
8 Schürmann, "Conditions of Evil," 391. The *Antigone* itself begins with an argument between Antigone and Ismene not simply about Antigone's intention to bury Polyneices, but her insistence not to keep it quiet, to speak it out and not to allow it to remain hidden. See Sophocles, *Antigone*, ed. Mark Griffith (Cambridge University Press, 1999), ll. 84–87.
9 Schürmann, "Conditions of Evil," 391.

tomb."[10] Antigone herself amplifies this when she refers to it as her "tomb, bridal chamber, permanent home dug of rock."[11] The manner in which the nuptial is intertwined here and throughout the play with mortality is not without significance for Schürmann's thinking, although he doesn't draw attention to it; for, as we will hear in chapter three, the image of the nuptial as it emerges in the poetry of René Char offers us a way to think, or imagine, the tension and union between the ultimate traits of natality and mortality.

Greek tragedy in general, and Sophocles' Oedipus cycle in particular, uncovers through the suffering of its characters, the irreconcilable connection between natality and mortality, and the tragic dimensions of every attempt to escape these ultimate conditions of human existence by positing and holding firm to some archic referent that would set things in order once and for all. The last words of Antigone speak of the suffering associated with her own piety, a reverence for the authority of the principle she has embraced from the beginning: "See what I suffer and from what man, because I gave reverence to the revered."[12] For Schürmann, this is the tragic suffering that enables us to understand, the *pathei mathos* of which Aeschylus speaks, and to which Schürmann appeals when emphasizing the way the thrust of archic normativity itself reveals the ultimate conditions of natality and mortality under which principles always operate. Schürmann puts it this way:

> There is no reconciliation between the ultimates of the universalizing impulse and the singularizing withdrawal. It will be a matter of examining how, from under the most solid normative constructions, the tragic pierces through. *Pathei*

---

10 Sophocles, *Antigone*, ll. 885–86. The Greek is *periptuxantes* (enfolding), which, as Griffith points out, is used "especially of human 'embraces', as well as military 'encirclement'." Ibid., 275. He points also to line 1237 where the marriage imagery persists.
11 Sophocles, *Antigone*, ll. 891–92.
12 Ibid., ll. 942–43.

mathos, "to suffer is to understand." How does this singularization that is *suffered* torment a *posited* sovereign?[13]

The suffering of which Antigone speaks points to the tragedy endemic to all reverence for hegemonic principles. In suffering with her through it, we are made to experience the manner in which the ultimate traits of natality and mortality "do not pair off." As Schürmann writes of these irreducible ultimates:

> They are originary, yet not binary traits. They are not jointly exhaustive of one genus. In other words, they do not divide one first posit that would yield to one encompassing discourse.... As incongruent, they derail experience.[14]

To learn to live a life conditioned by such incongruent traits without requiring recourse to some reassuring ultimate principle beyond or before them is, perhaps, the deepest lesson Schürmann had to teach.

Thus, what begins with Antigone ends with Oedipus at Colonus, the tragic figure who most eloquently stands for our human capacity to inhabit a world of differing ultimates. At the end of *Broken Hegemonies*, Schürmann suggests that it is "possible to enlarge one's way of thinking beyond the fantasied common."[15] He then gestures to Oedipus in posing the question of *Broken Hegemonies*: "With eyes opened by the hubristic sufferings that our age has inflicted on itself—as Oedipus at Colonus wants his eyes open and who thought of his eyes

---

13 Schürmann, *Broken Hegemonies*, 4. The appeal to *pathei mathos* refers to Aeschylus, J.D. Denniston, and Denys Lionel Page, *Agamemnon* (Oxford: Clarendon Press, 1960), l. 177.
14 Schürmann, "Conditions of Evil," 391.
15 Schürmann, *Broken Hegemonies*, 631. This sentence, importantly, includes a footnote to Kant's *Critique of Judgment*, sections 40 and 77 in which Kant identifies *die erweiterte Denkungsart*, the expanded way of thinking, with a sort of judgment that takes singulars into account. This way of thinking will be discussed in more detail in chapter four when we consider Schürmann's reading of Kant.

as open — is it possible to love the ultimates in differend?"[16] The interrogative heard here at the end of *Broken Hegemonies* is, however, in Schürmann's presentation at the conference on "The Politics of Transformation and the Limit of Imagination," declarative. On that fall September day in 1991, he had said: "it is possible to love differing ultimates." He then went on to suggest: "This, I submit, would be expanding the limits of imagination."[17]

The difference between these two passages can perhaps be explained in terms of Schürmann's attempt to adapt a text at home in a different context to an audience that had come to hear him speak to the question of politics and the imagination. Adapting oneself to one's audience is, of course, always good rhetorical practice; but it never occurs without philosophical significance, particularly for those of us who have learned the strategies of close reading Schürmann himself was at pains to teach. The shift in *Broken Hegemonies* from the declarative to the interrogative makes good sense at the end of a text that has sought to uncover the dangerous dynamics of thetic assertion itself. The interrogative form is less dogmatic, more open to the play of difference the book is designed to teach us how to "let be." But to extend the idea of thinking to an imagination expanding beyond its limits is a provocation that opens a path for us to follow as we attempt to discern the politics to which Schürmann's own thinking gestures.

This politics is poetic in nature, rooted in tragic ways of knowing most eloquently articulated in the stories of Aeschylus and Sophocles. At the beginning of *Broken Hegemonies*, Schürmann puts it this way:

> As we know, tragedy opens after disasters have already occurred, and nothing is left to be shown but the conditions that precipitated them. In Greece such a knowledge historically

---

16 Ibid. The "differend" names, for Schürmann, the irreducible conflict of ultimates. See ibid., 32. For a more detailed discussion of this technical term, see chapter 4.
17 Schürmann, "Conditions of Evil," 400.

preceded all doctrines of principles, and it is still necessary for us to retain it as the knowledge of a transgressive counter-strategy at work in every strategy that legislates simply.[18]

In the wake of the disasters of the 20th century and in the face of the challenges of the 21st, cultivating the habits of tragic thinking becomes urgent, indeed, imperative. But this requires, ultimately, the capacity to imagine and the cultivated commitment to love differing ultimates without recourse to another that is more fundamental and seemingly secure.

This, indeed, is the tragic knowledge that *Broken Hegemonies* seeks to teach. Schürmann returned to the stories of Sophocles and Aeschylus repeatedly, because Greek tragedy opens us to ways of recognizing the conditions under which principles are posited, reign, and wither. They uncover natality and mortality as the ultimate and irreducible conditions we must learn to love.

The Riddle of the Sphinx

In the Spring of 1991, a short essay on the last paintings of Louis Comtois was published in the art magazine, *Dialogue*. In it Schürmann writes eloquently and poignantly of the last and largest painting his longtime partner had created. It is called *The Riddle of the Sphinx: in the Morning on Four, at Noon on Two, in the Evening on Three*. The painting is, of course, a reference to the riddle Oedipus himself solved to become King of Thebes and husband to his own mother. It is a triptych, painted by a man who had died the year before in the early afternoon of life — at the age of forty-five on June 16, 1990, as Schürmann is careful to record it at the end of his essay.

Schürmann frames the essay, the last exhibition, and perhaps also the entirety of Comtois's oeuvre, as an insistent response to the nihilism of the 20th century. After the devastation we have inflicted upon one another, Schürmann asks, "has the night not fallen once and for all on the light of the beautiful in general and

---

18 Schürmann, *Broken Hegemonies*, 4.

on that of painted surfaces in particular?"[19] That this question involves philosophy as much as painting can be heard in the way Schürmann connects painting to thinking in this short essay: "'How to paint?' always depends on how one answers the prior question, 'How to think?'"[20]

In Comtois, Schürmann finds a different kind of thinking, one that embraces the light without refusing the darkness. Here then too, we encounter a way to love differing ultimates. *The Riddle of the Sphinx* and the answer to which it points — the painting and the life of a human-being — testify to the irreducible play of natality and mortality. Of the painting, Schürmann writes: "Beneath the bright, jubilant surface colours, there lies an undertow toward the dark; beneath the darkness, an incandescence."[21] The painting has depth and texture through the use of materials that give it, as Schürmann suggests, "the skin of a pachyderm," a living surface under which a certain luminosity persists.[22] However apt the description is of the painting, it also describes beautifully the depth and texture of Schürmann's own thinking in *Broken Hegemonies*. Beneath the darkness of the analytic of hegemonic ultimates, we are invited to attend to a certain luminosity, just as Oedipus, in his blindness, is finally empowered to see.

To discern this in *Broken Hegemonies*, we might attend to the appearance of Oedipus and Antigone in the text; for they embody the play of darkness and light, mortality and natality, that points not only to a different kind of thinking, but also to ways of imagining that gesture, in the end, to the transformative possibility of a poetic politics.

Tracing the appearances of Antigone and Oedipus in *Broken Hegemonies* will also enable us to paint in writing a kind of triptych of our own. Our triptych, like Comtois's, follows the structure of the riddle of the Sphinx. We begin in the morning, with Aristotle, who himself recognized more than Schürmann ever

---

19 Schürmann, "Dialogue," 6.
20 Ibid.
21 Ibid.
22 Ibid., 7.

gave him credit, the duplicity of beginning itself; in the afternoon, we turn to Plotinus where we find a gesture to the nuptial that offers us a way of imagining natality and mortality together without denying their irreducible difference; in the evening we turn to Kant, whose thinking more powerfully than perhaps any other gives voice to a *philosophy to come* rooted in mortal natality and its chiasmus, natal mortality—habits of being that empower us to love ultimates and teach us, in turn, to expand our imagination in ways that open us to new, more enriching ways of being together in a finite world.

"Life is death, and death also a life"

At the beginning and in the end, Schürmann speaks of Antigone and Oedipus. At the beginning, as we have heard, Antigone appears to introduce the phenomenon of the double bind, which for Schürmann is a situation that cannot be escaped by recourse to a third more primary obligation that would loosen the bonds of the two and allow for a kind of escape. Rather, the double bind must be suffered; it singularizes the individual bound. Antigone is caught between her obligations to her family and her obligations to her city; in choosing to bury her brother, she chooses to betray her king.

It is not, however, the choosing that singularizes Antigone, but the operation of the laws themselves, the way adherence to one always requires the withdrawal of the other, a withdrawal that never comes without consequences, however sophisticated our contrivances are to deny it. The hubris of Oedipus is rooted in the delusion of escape, for he thought he could avoid his destiny by fleeing Corinth, a flight that set him on a path to fulfill his horrible fate.

If, for Schürmann, Antigone stands for the manner in which principles singularize the individual "under one law, through a withdrawal toward the other,"[23] Oedipus stands for the manner in which tragic suffering opens a space for the individual be-

---
23 Schürmann, *Broken Hegemonies*, 4.

tween the thrust of the common necessary for life and the singularizing counter-thrust of mortality. The tenuous space of the individual, no longer singular but not yet particular, is ambiguous and difficult to inhabit. It is, as Schürmann says, "ravaged" by the thrust of natality and the undertow of mortality.[24] Yet it is the very space in which a poetic politics first becomes possible as a way of being rooted with myriad others in the ravaged site between natality and mortality.

For Schürmann, Oedipus inhabits just such a site after his eyes have been opened by the blinding realization of his tragic situation. Hölderlin put it this way in his poem, *In lieblicher Bläue…*:

> King Oedipus has, perhaps, an eye too many. These sufferings of this man, they seem indescribable, unspeakable, inexpressible. Which comes when drama represents such things…. The sufferings of Oedipus seem like a poor man lamenting what he lacks. Son of Laios, poor stranger in Greece! Life is death, and death is also a life.[25]

Sometimes, of course, the inexpressible finds expression nonetheless in poetry. The tragic sufferings of Oedipus in *Oedipus at Colonus* seem here to be just that, the expression of the ineffable fate of a man who has become a stranger in his homeland, and yet, who inhabits a ravaged site with "an eye too many," aware now finally of the tragic situation that conditions his life.

According to Schürmann, Sophocles gives voice to this awareness in *Oedipus at Colonus,* when Oedipus approaches the site of his own death, a place to which he points and which itself points to a kind of silence.

> He sees and knows that for which there is no fantasm: that singular object of monstration, his death (and, advancing toward its place, Oedipus *points it out* to Theseus). The

---

24 Ibid., 16.
25 Friedrich Hölderlin, *Hymns and Fragments*, trans. Richard Sieburth (Princeton: Princeton University Press, 1984), 252.

> singularizing withdrawal that death exerts on life would reduce language to zero if it were possible for us to see it in all its clarity. A radical *Aufklärung* on the subject of fantasms would deprive us of the common space where the give and take of speech proves to us that we are not dead.[26]

Politics, rooted in the give and take of speech, is proof we are not dead. It is not possible for us to see mortality in all its clarity; even a blind Oedipus must resort to language up until the final moment, and even then, he has recourse to the demonstrative act of pointing that is enough of a speech act to maintain the community he has established with Theseus. The power of the demonstrative comes to language too in Hölderlin when he speaks of "these sufferings of this man" to draw attention to the condition of the individual who finds expression in Sophoclean poetry as Oedipus.

"In tragedy," Schürmann writes, "silence enters the domain of the gesture."[27] The gesture points, for Schürmann, to the ravaged site between birth and death, to the place where language emerges from and recedes back to silence, to the site, that is, between natality and mortality where politics unfolds. In *Broken Hegemonies,* Oedipus, particularly as he appears in *Oedipus at Colonus,* is the figure who helps us learn something of how to inhabit this ravaged site.

This site itself is determined by the existential conditions of natality and mortality. Natality, Schürmann insists, is the trait of new beginnings, of language, and of institutions. It is the trait under which communities are established. But it is also the trait of delusion and domination, "this trait crushes the singular."[28] The totalizing dimension of natality emerges when it is presumed to be unfettered by mortality. As Schürmann writes, "But in denying mortality, this trait steers straight into metaphysical theticism."[29]

---

26 Schürmann, *Broken Hegemonies,* 18.
27 Ibid., 35.
28 Ibid., 19.
29 Ibid.

At Colonus, Oedipus appears to have relinquished the delusions of his own birth: having been blinded by hubris, he now sees, perhaps, indeed, with "an eye too many." He has come to terms with his own finitude; embraced mortality, the trait of dissolution, of silence, and of destitution. It is the trait through which we are separated from one another. But it is also the trait of authenticity and liberation; it "familiarizes us with our *singularization to come*"[30] on the basis of which another kind of politics emerges, one that is not rooted in hegemonic fantasms or predicated on archic domination.

"By virtue of mortality, *the future solifies*, by virtue of natality, *it totalizes*."[31] Between them, politics emerges as poetic play, a kind of making together capable of delight and oriented by the unfolding of truth, a way of being together with others that is as acutely aware of our tendencies to totalize as it is accepting of our inevitable demise. This sense of poetics will be developed further in the next chapter when we consider Aristotle and the duplicity of beginning. For now, however, the figure of Oedipus at Colonus points to the contours of the topology of poetic politics by suggesting how it might be possible to inhabit a site determined decisively by what Schürmann calls the *differend*.[32] In a dense but important passage that might best be unpacked in stages, Schürmann charts the contours of the topology of a poetic politics:

---

30 Ibid.
31 Ibid.
32 The figure of Oedipus at Colonus seems to haunt *Broken Hegemonies* whenever it attempts to put words to the idea of the *differend*. It is introduced in the context of Greek tragedy and its truth is said to be seen by Oedipus, see ibid., 28. Later, the differend *binds* us "— like Oedipus blinded and sophos — to the excess of light that is also night" (135). And in the end, when Schürmann backs away, as we will see, from the language of differend, he appeals both to Antigone and to *Oedipus at Colonus*, although there in a way that is wrapped up with a potentially disturbing apologetic for Heidegger's alleged "sudden awakening in the mid-1930's." In a strange way that must be considered carefully, the idea of the *differend* in Schürmann is also haunted by the specter of Heidegger and his disastrous political engagement with National Socialism.

Our singularization to come has expelled us in advance from our every insertion into a world — we say from every constituted phenomenality. Singularization dephenomenalizes.

The thrust of mortality is emphasized here; the insistence on destitution must be maintained if the totalizing tendencies of natality are not to be permitted to reign supreme. Because *Broken Hegemonies* remains concerned throughout with tracing the delusions of natality as they articulate themselves in the hegemonic fantasms of Western history and philosophy, it repeatedly returns to the condition of mortality to hold our attempts to establish community accountable to that which dephenomenalizes. The emphasis on destitution is further amplified as the passage unfolds:

> Topology teaches us what binds us in every normative position, not just what is represented as maximal, but also the deictic experience from which it was extracted and which will come to haunt it, destitute it.

This topological teaching points to a tenuous bind; yet it is a binding nonetheless, one infused with its own destitution to such an extent that any attempt to cover over that which haunts our relationships with one another — the pull of mortality itself — succumbs to the delusion of stability that inevitably gives rise to injustice, violence, and domination.

Here Schürmann finds a mere affirmation of difference too anemic to describe the rich dynamics of the conditions under which politics unfold:

> The vocabulary of difference does not express very well the ultimates which make us posit the *koinon* and let the *deiktikon* be. If it is as mortals that we know how the undertow toward the monstrable singular always works on demon-

strable theses, then the strategies crossing each other in the event, instead, maintain a *differend*.[33]

Natality enjoins us to posit the common, mortality requires us to let the demonstrable be. The topology of political life requires us to learn how to live in and with a *differend*.

Agamemnon refused it in his decision to murder his daughter; or perhaps more precisely, in the tragic denial that enabled him to live with himself in the wake of that fateful decision.[34] The univocal law, born in denial, is sustained by delusion. The hegemonic fantasms *Broken Hegemonies* is designed to trace follow this pattern of denial and delusion. Yet, the book itself is not only a symptomatology;[35] and even if it is also not strictly speaking prescriptive — for that too would fall into the dysfunctional normative-legislative pattern the book helps us diagnose and escape — it is therapeutic.

The path of amelioration to which Schürmann points may be discerned in the figure of Oedipus as he appears at Colonus. The site he inhabits after the hubris and the denial and the blinding recognition is the site of the human condition laid bare; a place riven by a differend that is by definition irreconcilable: the thrust of natality and the undertow of mortality. As Schürmann writes, "Thus the differend reveals its originary site."[36] Here the difference between what is said and what shows itself requires

---

33 Ibid., 26.
34 Long, "The Daughters of Metis."
35 A symptomological approach identifies moments of disruption that show themselves in a text. Emanuela Bianchi, a student of Schürmann's, has emphasized the connection with the Greek word *sumptōma*, to suggest that a symptom "signifies a fundamental disruption of hierarchy and teleology." See Emanuela Bianchi, *The Feminine Symptom: Aleatory Matter in the Aristotelian Cosmos*, 1st edn. (New York: Fordham University Press, 2014), 9. *Broken Hegemonies* is also a symptomology, for it points to the disruption endemic to the hegemonic operation of principles. But it also moves beyond the symptom to the diagnosis and, thus, points to a path of amelioration. To be clear, however, amelioration is not cure; for there is no cure for the conditions under which life itself operates.
36 Schürmann, *Broken Hegemonies*, 36.

attention and care; for in the remainder the possibility of a kind of community opens itself to humans capable of inhabiting such a ravaged site.

Schürmann points to this remainder, which itself plays a demonstrative function in pointing to a place where a different kind of politics might unfold. "The differend between the enunciative and the ostensive exhibits its violence as it severs what we say from the 'this' that can only be pointed to with a finger."[37] As will be shown, the "this" to which Schürmann points here comes to poignant language in Aristotle's enunciation of the *tode ti*, an articulation of that which shows itself no longer as singular but not yet as particular — the individual situated in a site ravaged by natality and mortality.

This is precisely the site that Oedipus inhabits at Colonus. Importantly, however, he is not alone in having learned to live in such a ravaged site, for his daughters, Antigone and Ismene, inhabit it with him. Together Antigone and Oedipus, exiled and wandering, and later, joining them, Ismene, have learned to be somehow at home in a place that Schürmann himself thematizes is the very site in which the human condition unfolds:

> The one certainty of mortals is that there is a differend between *this*, which is taking place before us, and what we say about it; between Oedipus seized by just anger against an insolent charioteer and an Oedipus thereby falling first under Labdacian and later under Theban laws; between everydayness and the fantasm that frames it; between a given being and being fantasized as order.... Don't forget that under the legislative denial of Oedipus, Thebes was made livable once again! The differend, then, constitutes the human condition — a condition in the sense of a critical transcendentalism that recognizes in fractured being — a being that breaks us — the "first known" whose evidence philosophers have always had the mission to demonstrate.[38]

---

37 Ibid., 35.
38 Ibid., 36.

The differend conditions human life. It is at once the possible site of denial that establishes a place as livable — though only for a time (for legislative denial always carries within it the seeds of its own destruction); but it is also the possible site of a differend recognized, a space inhabitable without that denial which sets the hegemonic operation of principles into motion, a site ravaged and yet capable of a kind of gathering. To habituate ourselves to such a ravaged site is no easy task, indeed, it may perhaps be the task of an entire life; and yet there are Antigone and Ismene with Oedipus at Colonus, depending upon one another, holding each other up nonetheless: "Antigone and Oedipus are not victims 'crushed by the terrible wheel of fate'; they live the dissolution at the core of every consolidation, and they affirm it."[39]

We are here on the trail of the core teaching of Schürmann's thinking, a teaching that was only dimly discernable to me on that fall September day in 1991 when I first heard Schürmann speak of the dangers of metaphysical theticism. The desire to posit something firm and foundational is rooted in our inability to inhabit the ravaged site that conditions our existence. Metaphysics is "boring" because it repeats the pathological tendency to posit principles as ultimate and then to pretend that somehow those principles have an ultimacy independent of our decision to posit them. Somehow Oedipus, Antigone, and Ismene learned to inhabit the ravaged site that conditions mortal life without recourse to such metaphysical positing. This is one reason, it seems, that Schürmann returned to *Oedipus at Colonus* regularly throughout *Broken Hegemonies* at precisely those moments when the positing of principles has been exhausted and space is opened for us to discern the ravaged site to which the text itself points as a possible place of politics.

---

39 Ibid., 134. As will be heard in the end, Ismene too affirms the dissolution ¾ but her presence is eclipsed by Schürmann, as is Antigone herself when Schürmann focuses on the figure of Oedipus at Colonus. The long legacy of patriarchal individualism is here at work on Schürmann despite everything and not without irony, for Schürmann himself has done much to help us unlearn the hegemonic fantasms of the patriarch.

Referring to *Oedipus at Colonus*, Schürmann writes: "In this tragedy, the most difficult for us moderns to understand, all questioning has ceased. Discordance has been accepted, even affirmed, and it breaks the hero."[40] An important shift can be heard here, one it will be important to mark and attend to as we proceed to uncover the ravaged site *Broken Hegemonies* invites us to inhabit.

The analytic of ultimates undertaken by *Broken Hegemonies* uncovers those moments of diremption that signal the disparate unfolding of being itself.[41] Here we will trace the diremption of being in Aristotle, Plotinus, and Kant. Schürmann, however, also finds it poignantly expressed in Heidegger's attempts to give voice to the happening of being as an event in the *Beiträge zur Philosophie*. In Heidegger, Schürmann finds a reading of the history of philosophy that "shows that we have always lived under the *historical differing* where conflictuality remains tragic because it is deprived of any adjudicating fantasm."[42]

Those moments of diremption, Schürmann insists, "are so many manners in which the incongruity of death is adjoined to life." Here he goes on to shift his vocabulary from the "differend" to "discordance."

> Strictly speaking, the undertow it exerts no longer gives rise to a differend, but to a discordance — if at least by differend one understand[s] the conflict of disparate laws calling for an impossible common authority. I speak of a differend only to

---

40 Ibid., 552. Intentionally omitted here is how Schürmann's text continues to establish an analogy between Oedipus and Heidegger after his own tragic failing. Heidegger is a critical figure for Schürmann, always, but especially at the end of *Broken Hegemonies*. In refusing to follow Schürmann in this analogy, I hope to resist falling into a kind of apologetics for Heidegger. Here, the interest is Oedipus, not Heidegger.

41 For the technical sense of "diremption" as that which "signifies the loss of every hegemony," see ibid., 623. This is discussed in further detail in chapter 5.

42 Ibid., 550.

describe this call and the referents that are posited to fulfill it in an illusory manner."[43]

In *Oedipus at Colonus* at least, Oedipus, Antigone, and Ismene seem to have relinquished the pathologies of the differend, if as Schürmann suggests, this term is deployed to refer to a call for stability that is met with a thetic, and thus delusional, response. Oedipus, Antigone, and Ismene inhabit a site conditioned by discordance, a term that perhaps better resonates with the dissonance endemic to the play of natality and mortality.

Schürmann sees Oedipus inhabiting this site, but he also fails to see Antigone there with him, let alone her sister, Ismene, who appears too with them at Colonus. The symbolic power of these three there together uncovers dimensions of the poetics of politics to which we will, in the end, return, for Sophocles gives voice there to a gathering conditioned by a thrust of natality that does not deny the counter-thrust of mortality, an eloquence in discord.

But this eloquence, symbolized by the touching relationship between Antigon, Ismene, and Oedipus at Colonus, Schürmann tends to elide. Rather, he emphasizes the experience of the patriarch who

> has accepted who he is: not the dispenser of justice who saved Thebes, but the defiler who brought it to the verge of ruin. He made its fateful destiny his own. Unhappy for having denied the ancestral allegiance, he then becomes happy because of his belonging to the fateful fissuring of the ancestral and the civil laws, gratified with apotheosis, and enthroned as the patron hero of Athens.[44]

To turn our attention to his status as patron hero is to shift focus from the fateful fissuring he learned to inhabit with his daughters. It is to repeat the compulsion to posit the patriarch as hero,

---

43 Ibid., 551.
44 Ibid., 583.

the symbol of ultimate hegemonic authority. In this sense, it is a reading of the tragedy that fails to live up to the hermeneutical approach Schürmann himself sought to teach.[45] How such a co-habitation is possible will be addressed in chapter five, where a reading that is not blind to the relationship between Oedipus and his daughters will be developed. For now, however, the story of Oedipus at Colonus has set us on a path that enables us to discern the contours of a politics to which Schürmann, like Sophocles, gestures without articulating how it might be put into practice.

The path to which Schürmann here points requires us to follow a thread that runs through the analytic of ultimates *Broken Hegemonies* uncovers. Along the way, we will not attempt to provide a full account of the text or even to capture all of the rich nuance of the analytic itself. Rather, we will remain focused on the politics to which Schürmann points without fully developing. The analytic of ultimates uncovers the limits of hegemonic thinking, the dangers of metaphysical theticism. This is an important place to begin; indeed, it was precisely the alluring place a number of us began with Schürmann in the fall of 1991. But beginnings, as we will see in the next chapter, are duplicitous. As we start down the path of critique, we soon find ourselves presented with new possibilities that open once old modes of thinking and acting are revealed as pathologically destructive.

We begin, then, with Aristotle, a thinker who understood more than Schürmann gave him credit for, the duplicitous operation of inception. This will lead, in turn, to Plotinus, whom Schürmann taught us to read as marking the end of the ancient hegemony of the one. By bringing Schürmann's innovative and compelling reading of René Char's poem, *The Shark and the Gull*, into dialogue with Plotinus we come to encounter the power of symbols to transform reality and open us to new constellations of possible community. In Plotinus, where we expected to en-

---

45 For a discussion of Schürmann's practices of reading, see Christopher P. Long, "Care of Death: On the Teaching of Reiner Schürmann," *Philosophy Today*, January 31, 2017, 351–63.

counter an end, we experience a new way of thinking natality in terms of what comes to language in Char as the nuptial. Having thus been awakened to the power of symbols, we are prepared to experience how in Kant being itself comes to expression as plurivocal in a way that reveals just how pathologically delusional it is to attempt to deploy univocal principles in a plurivocal world. This opens us to what Schürmann calls the "singularization to come," a formulation that gestures to a mode of comportment at home in the ravaged site between natality and mortality. This will, then, return us to Oedipus at Colonus; but not to him alone. Rather, it points to the relationship that emerges for a time between Antigone, Ismene, and Oedipus, as they navigate a way between their exile from Thebes and Oedipus's final resting place near Athens. Here, having been awakened to the power of a poetic politics, we attend to three symbolic moments of touching between Oedipus and his daughters through which we might discern something of the new possibilities a poetic politics opens for us if we settle into the ravaged site that conditions our existence, together.

2

Morning
The Duplicity of Beginning

Do not wish to be master in everything,
for the things you mastered did not
    accompany you throughout your
life.
            — Sophocles, *Oedipus Tyrannus,* Creon, ll. 1522–23.¹

Beginnings are poetic.² They are haunted by an ineluctable duplicity that is heard already in the Greek word *poiēsis*. On one hand, poiesis names the sort of making associated with fabrication, on the other, it points to the creative capacity to imitate action in a way that brings delight and discloses truth.³ This duplicity of *poiēsis* haunts the story Reiner Schürmann tells of the

---

1 Sophocles, *Sophoclis Fabulae* (Oxford: Clarendon Press, 1990).
2 An earlier version of this chapter was originally published as Christopher P. Long, "The Duplicity of Beginning: Schürmann, Aristotle and the Origins of Metaphysics," *The Graduate Faculty Philosophy Journal* 29, no. 2 (2008).
3 For the second sense of *poiēsis*, see Aristotle and Rudolf Kassel, *Aristotelis De Arte Poetica Liber* (Oxford: E Typographeo Clarendoniano, 1966), 1448b4–9. Hereafter, *Poetics*. There Aristotle locates the two natural causes of the poetic capacity (*poiētikē*) in the co-natural tendency to imitate in human-beings and in the delight humans take in imitations. In the Sophist, the activity of *mimēsis* is associated with the capacity to disclose the true proportions of things. See Plato, *Platonis Opera,* vol. 1 (New York: Oxford University Press, 1995), 235c–e.

beginning of metaphysics in his book *Heidegger on Being and Acting: From Principles to Anarchy*. Metaphysics is said to begin with a decisive determination of the very meaning of beginning. Indeed, it is said to begin with a certain *poiēsis*, a fabrication that systematically undermines the other sense of *poiēsis* that speaks of possible things and opens a space for the happening of truth.[4] For Schürmann, Aristotle was the poet of the beginning of metaphysics, because he was the first to bring together the two senses of the Greek word *archē*, inception and domination, consolidating them into a single concept of the principle in which incipience gives way to domination as the univocal law that governs thinking and acting.[5]

Ironically, Schürmann's own account of the origin of metaphysics repeats the consolidation of the origin he associates with Aristotle. For Schürmann, metaphysics "designates that disposition where action requires a principle to which words, things and deeds can be related."[6] To identify an expression that captures this schema by which action is determined by a universal principle of domination, Schürmann appeals to the Aristotelian locution of *pros hen* equivocation in which a diversity of phenomena enter into community with one another by pointing toward one (*pros hen*) principle, or *archē*.[7] Although, as will be heard, Aristotle's own account of *pros hen* equivocation cannot be reduced to the hegemonic operation of the one upon the many, the logic that drives the story Schürmann tells

---

4 Heidegger emphasizes this second sense of poiesis when he speaks of poiesis as the "setting-itself-into-work of truth." See Martin Heidegger, "Der Ursprung Des Kunstwerkes," in *Holzwege* (Frankfurt am Main: Vittorio Klostermann, 1994), 59. For an English translation, see Martin Heidegger, *Poetry, Language, Thought*, trans. Albert Hofstadter (New York: Harper and Row, 1971), 72. The second sense of *poiēsis* is heard already in Aristotle as well when he insists in the *Poetics* that poetry speaks of possible things and of the whole. *Poetics*, 1451a30–b10.

5 Reiner Schürmann, *Heidegger on Being and Acting: From Principles to Anarchy* (Bloomington: Indiana University Press, 1987), 97.

6 Ibid., 5–6.

7 Aristotle, *Aristotelis Metaphysica* (Oxford: Oxford University Press, 1992), IV.2, 1003b5.

about the origin of metaphysics forces him, not quite to deny, but certainly to underemphasize the degree to which in Aristotle the *pros hen* relation affirms difference. Schürmann's story of the origin of metaphysics as an epoch of hegemonic principles is itself a fabrication that operates according to a logic of domination that elides those dimensions of the beginning dissonant with the narrative.[8]

Thus, to begin with Schürmann is to be exposed to the poetic duplicity of beginning in a poignant way; for his is a singular thinking intent upon exposing the violence each new beginning perpetrates upon the singular itself. To begin with Schürmann is to be caught already in a double bind in which the very attempt to do justice to the singularity of his thinking requires the deployment of words that obliterate the singular by forcing it into an economy of concepts that renders it particular. Yet justice requires that we resist the temptation to do with Schürmann what he does with Aristotle; for the singularity of Aristotle's thinking is rendered particular the moment Schürmann identifies him as the father of metaphysics. Every attempt to do justice to singularity is caught up in the poetic duplicity of beginning — the need to speak and act together and the violence endemic to such speaking and acting. This is the duplicity that Schürmann himself identifies as the condition under which life stretches itself out between natality and mortality.

Drawing explicitly on one aspect of Hannah Arendt's discussion of natality in the *Human Condition*, Schürmann insists that the trait of natality not only "carries us toward new beginnings,"[9] but more decisively, natality gives birth to principles that crush

---

8   We might playfully suggest, with a glint of delight in the eye, that Schürmann's own account of the origins of metaphysics is ... metaphysical and "very, very bo-o-oring." Even so, however, his account is neither unimportant nor unproductive, for it generated a poietic response of sorts in two of his students: see, Christopher P. Long and Richard A. Lee, "Between Reification and Mystification: Rethinking the Economy of Principles," *Telos* 120 (2001): 92–112.

9   Reiner Schürmann, *Broken Hegemonies*, trans. Reginald Lilly (Bloomington: Indiana University Press, 2003), 18.

the singular.¹⁰ Natality names the thetic thrust at work in every act of institutional founding. But what gives this life-affirming condition tragic poignancy for Schürmann is the manner in which its activity denies mortality. If "mortality familiarizes us with our *singularization to come*," natality wins a life for itself by forcing the singular under concepts that render it particular.¹¹ For Schürmann, then, the trait of natality is associated with life, the common, and the violence of language, while that of mortality is bound up with death, the singular, and a certain silence.¹²

However, to posit natality as the exclusive trait under which the singular dissolves into particularity and to set it over against the trait of mortality as that which singularizes is to remain caught in a metaphysical logic of dichotomy that Schürmann himself does so much to call into question. Unless these traits themselves are integrated, woven into "the entire tragedy and comedy of life," the distinction is destined to remain one more in a long line of metaphysical phantasms.¹³ The singularizing dimension of natality must be heard to stretch out into the universalizing function of mortality. Natality opens us to the singular as the source of new possibilities even as mortality presses

---

10 Ibid., 19. For an insightful discussion of natality in *Broken Hegemonies*, see Reginald Lilly, "The Topology of *Des Hégémonies brisées*," *Research in Phenomenology* 28 (1998): 226–42, at 234. The passage from the Human Condition that seems decisive for Schürmann's understanding of natality runs as follows: "The frailty of human institutions and laws and, generally, of all matter pertaining to men's living together, arises from the human condition of natality and is quite independent of the frailty of human nature." See Hannah Arendt, *The Human Condition* (Chicago: University of Chicago Press, 1958), 191. Cf. Schürmann, *Broken Hegemonies*, 635n33. What Schürmann sometimes seems to underplay is the extent to which natality itself carries with it singularity in Arendt: "The fact that man is capable of action means that the unexpected can be expected from him, that he is able to perform what is infinitely improbable. And this again is possible only because each man is unique, so that with each birth something uniquely new comes into the world." See Arendt, *The Human Condition*, 178.
11 Schürmann, *Broken Hegemonies*, 19.
12 Ibid.
13 Plato, *Platonis Opera*, vol. II (Oxford: Oxford University Press, 1901), *Philebus*, 50b2.

in upon life indiscriminately. If the tragic names the mode in which the bonds of mortality singularize, perhaps comedy is the mode in which natality playfully bursts the totalizing bonds of mortality, not by "teaching the end of bonds," but by opening a space for the emergence of new possibilities for thinking and acting. This space of appearance, conditioned as much by natality as by mortality, is the *topos* in which the individual — situated precariously between the singular and the particular — comes to presence. The site of the individual's appearance is the one toward which (*pros hen*) thinking and acting must always return if they are to temper their own hegemonic tendencies and cultivate an ability to respond in ways that do justice to the appearing of things. Schürmann's intense focus on combating the tragic denial that annihilates the singular itself eclipses the perplexing appearance of the individual at play in the space between singularity and particularity. Here a comic denial can be heard in the way the preoccupation with the tragic reinforces a long history of philosophy's obsession with death to the detriment of life.

Let us begin again, then, with Schürmann in order first to attend to the manner in which the logic of domination at work in his narrative of the origin of metaphysics suppresses the singular poetics of Aristotelian thinking. To hear the duplicity of that beginning is already to begin to feel the play of natality and mortality that operate together in each new beginning. This will allow us to hear more clearly how Schürmann's analysis of natality in its relation to mortality in *Broken Hegemonies* opens the possibility of reading Aristotle's thinking as something other than the origin of an errancy. In *Broken Hegemonies,* this other Aristotle is permitted to speak and it is Aristotle's peculiar ways of speaking that allows the individual to appear between the silence of singularity and the violence of particularity. Aristotle's own phenomenological orientation to the ways things are said allows the things said to open a site in which the possibility of a certain justice emerges.[14]

Metaphysics as Poetic Fantasm

Aristotle's *Physics* is said to be the foundational book of Western metaphysics because it transforms the inquiry into the first beginnings (*archai*) of nature into a search for causes. This shift covers over the original sense of nature as *phusis*, a noun that retains its intimate link to the verb (*phuein*), to come forth into appearance. The attempt to articulate the beginnings of the dynamic event that is nature's appearing is eclipsed by an obsession with locating those causes that stand at the beginning of a chain of responsibility capable of answering the metaphysical question *par excellence*, why?, or *dia ti*, through what? For Schürmann, the human fetish for fabrication perverts the inquiry into origins into a search for causes. He puts it this way: "[I]t is only because man first grasps himself as archi-tect, as initiator of fabrication, that nature can in turn appear to him as moved by the mechanisms of cause and effect."[15] Aristotle's *Physics* introduces the four causes in order to account not merely for the sort of change at work in human making, but, as Aristotle insists, for "every natural change."[16] For Schürmann, the attempt to extend the model of production to all natural change can be heard in the very examples to which Aristotle appeals in establishing the

---

14 For a detailed reading of Aristotle from this phenomenological perspective, see Christopher P. Long, *Aristotle on the Nature of Truth* (New York: Cambridge University Press, 2011).

15 Schürmann, *Heidegger on Being and Acting*, 100. Schürmann explicitly references Nietzsche's *Will to Power*, section 551 for the notion that the concept of causality is anthropocentric, derived from our own ability to manipulate things.

16 Aristotle links the discussion of the causes (*aitiai*) to the why question and the why question to a certain eidenai, or knowledge at *Physics*, II.3, 194b17–23. See Aristotle, *Aristotelis Physica* (Oxford, England: Oxford University Press, 1992). There he insists that the search for causes must be about "both coming into being and passing away and about every natural change (*metabolē*)...."

material, formal, efficient, and final causes, most of which are taken from the sphere of human fabrication or action.[17]

The shift that thinks nature in terms of human fabrication is decisive for Schürmann's account of the origin of metaphysics, because it illustrates how the model of production gives rise to an obsession with causes that comes to color our understanding of action in general and political action in particular. The drive to lead all principles of being back to ultimate causes gives rise to the tendency to conceive action in terms of ultimate rules and laws and to reduce politics to obedience. Yet, to trace this trajectory in Aristotle from the *Physics* to the *Politics*, Schürmann leads us along a rather convoluted path too quickly. He appeals first to that provocative and enigmatic passage at the end of the *Posterior Analytics*, in which Aristotle suggests that a principle arises from perception in a manner similar to the way "a reversal in battle is generated (*genomenēs*) when one man makes a stand, then another, then another, until they attain a principle."[18] Taking this passage out of the context in which it is found — namely, as part of an attempt to account for how the principles of demonstrations are acquired — Schürmann thematizes it as an illustration of "the constitution of a principle for action."[19] He goes on to insist:

> The entire army does not stop because two or three master their fear but suddenly it obeys orders again and the activity of each become again the action of all. Aristotle views command (*archē*) imposing its order on the runaways just as he views substance, as *archē*, imposing its unity upon the accidents. Such is the filiation between ousiology and practical

---

17 Schürmann recognizes that the examples that illustrate the formal cause — the two-to-one ratio of the octave and number in general — are exceptions. See Schürmann, *Heidegger on Being and Acting*, 329n32.
18 *Post. An.*, II.19, 100a12–3. See Aristotle, *Aristotelis Analytica Priora et Posteriora* (Oxford: Oxford University Press, 1964).
19 Schürmann, *Heidegger on Being and Acting*, 39.

philosophy. Both observations are construed in relation "to the one."[20]

Yet the text of the *Posterior Analytics* speaks of a reversal in battle "being generated" (*genomenēs*), a term that evokes not the imposition of order by a principle external to the order, but the coming-into-being of order from within. Morphologically, the Greek verb *gignesthai*, is a middle deponent: having an active voice only in the perfect tense.[21] In it, therefore, the force of the middle voice must be heard. Schürmann himself recognizes the middle voice as undermining the hegemony of a dichotomous thinking that posits a simple disjunction between agent and patient.[22] Yet Schürmann's own reading of the turning in battle stifles the dimension of the middle voice that resonates in the deponent verb. The example of the reversal, whatever its other limitations, does not suggest that the army turns because it begins again to obey orders from outside and above. Rather, an order comes into being from within the army itself, as one of its organic parts turns, lending courage to others. To read this text as an example of the imposition of a hegemonic principle and to put it in the service of an account of how the principle of action is constituted, performs a double — we might even say, duplicitous — violence: it at once abstracts the example from the context to which it belongs and imposes upon it a reading domi-

---

20 Ibid.
21 With *gignesthai*, the first, second, third and fifth principle parts are taken from the middle voice, the perfect stem is an active form. The problem of how to think generation is built into the morphology of this Greek verb. The active and passive dimensions of the verb resonate in this middle deponent. In English, as Smyth insists, the middle deponent is simply registered in the active voice. See Herbert Weir Smyth, *Greek Grammar* (Cambridge: Harvard University Press, 1956), 107. Schürmann's recognition that modern languages, even when they render the middle in terms of reflexivity, stifle middle voice is even more pronounced with the middle deponent, for the active meaning mutes the middle voice yet further.
22 Schürmann writes: "Beneath the self-affirmation of the grammatical subject and the institution of a normative-nominative system, it is necessary to see — or rather to hear — the very stifling of the middle voice." See Schürmann, *Broken Hegemonies*, 38–39.

nated by the trope of imposition. The reading is, quite literally, a fabrication. It enframes the text, taking it as standing-reserve for a poetic fable about the beginning of metaphysics as dominated by an obsession with production.[23]

The fable becomes fantasmic as the trope of imposition is imposed first upon the fundamental, ontological relation between substance (*ousia*) and its accidents, and then extended yet further to practical philosophy in general by means of an interpretation of the *pros hen* relation that is itself governed by an obsession with domination. If Schürmann deploys the term "hegemony" to name the attempt to posit a norm according to which a diversity of phenomena are set in order and, further, if this thetic maneuver becomes a "fantasm" the moment it is itself effaced so that the hegemonic ordering may be legitimized as the natural order of things, then perhaps Schürmann's own reading of Aristotle, which posits production as the law according to which the Aristotelian corpus is set in order, can itself be said to be a hegemonic fantasm.[24]

And yet, there is in this story of beginning, as with every poetic beginning, a certain instability that announces itself in the very moment of its institution. To discern this instability, it will be necessary to begin again with Aristotle, in order to

---

[23] The vocabulary here, of course, is meant to call to mind Heidegger's essay *Die Frage nach der Technik,* and particularly the meaning of *das Gestell* (enframing) and *Bestand* (standing-reserve). For the German, see Martin Heidegger, *Die Technik und Die Kehre* (Pfullingen: Verlag Günther Neske, 1991), 16–23. The English can be found in Martin Heidegger, *The Question Concerning Technology, and Other Essays,* trans. William Levitt (New York: Harper Torchbooks, 1977), 17–23.

[24] Schürmann introduces the notion of a fantasm early in *Broken Hegemonies*: "Fantasms rule by authorizing not the deduction of a finite corpus of conclusions, but the indefinite association of representations that require that one follow them …. Hence, if laws are measured against the fantasmic authority, then this fantasmic authority will be normative in the sense that one refers to it as the law of laws." See Schürmann, *Broken Hegemonies,* 6. He goes on to develop the meaning of hegemony in relation to fantasm: "A fantasm is hegemonic when an entire culture relies on it as if it provided that in the name of which one speaks and acts" See ibid., 7. See also Lilly, "The Topology of *Des Hégémonies brisées,*" 236.

attempt yet another beginning with Schürmann. Aristotle's thinking does not consolidate itself into a systematic totality of thought centered upon the single experience of fabrication. Although there remains in Aristotle a tendency to appeal to examples taken from "the region of manipulable things" for heuristic purposes,[25] Aristotle's thinking is peripatetic and phenomenological. He remains committed throughout to living in intimate association with the phenomena of nature and his thinking is for this reason, itinerant. It will be necessary then, to follow a path of Aristotelian thinking concerning the meaning of *ousia* in order to discern an itinerary guided more by a loyalty to the perplexing phenomenon that is *ousia* than by an attempt to impose upon it the structure of fabrication. Tracing this path of thinking will allow us to return to Schürmann's story of the beginning of metaphysics in order to discern the extent to which another beginning is recognized but suppressed.

The Poetics of Aristotelian Thinking

Aristotle's thinking is borne by a tension that gives it life; for it is a thinking conditioned by a profound sense of what Socrates in the *Philebus* calls the "entire tragedy and comedy of life."[26] In that text, the comic is associated with the exposure of pretense and, in particular, with the pretense of those who, unable to adhere to the Delphic admonition, "Know Thyself," become ridiculous by professing a knowledge accessible only to the divine. [27] The comic, then, like the tragic, is a way of responding

---

25 For a discussion of the heuristic importance of the appeal to artifacts as examples see, Christopher P. Long, *The Ethics of Ontology: Rethinking an Aristotelian Legacy* (Albany: State University of New York Press, 2004), 32–33 and 174n3. Michael Ferejohn too emphasizes the manner in which Aristotle appeals to artifacts for heuristic purposes. See Michael Ferejohn, "The Definition of Generated Composites," in *Unity, Identity, and Explanation in Aristotle's Metaphysics,* eds.Theodore Scaltsas, David Charles, and Mary Louise Gill (Oxford: Clarendon Press, 1994), 296n.
26 *Philebus,* 50b2.
27 *Philebus,* 48c–51a. See too, William Chase Greene, "The Spirit of Comedy in Plato," *Harvard Studies in Classical Philology* 31 (1920): 63–123, at 67. Drew

to the finitude that conditions life; but unlike the tragic, which involves always a denial of ultimate conditions, the comic is intent on exposing these conditions, celebrating them, despite themselves, as the very conditions under which the possibility of community unfolds.

The tension endemic to "the whole tragedy and comedy of life" at work in Aristotle's thinking can be heard already in the way he articulates the situation that conditions philosophy as a search for truth:

> The investigation concerning truth is in one sense difficult, in another sense easy. ... So if it seems that we happen to be in the condition of the common saying, 'who could miss the doorway?,' in this way it would be easy, but to have the whole in a certain way (*to d'holon ti echein*), and yet not to be capable of part of it, shows the difficulty of it.[28]

The path of truth is an open door. To miss the doorway is to close oneself to the play of possibility that reveals the truth of things. And yet, this openness, this playful accessibility, suggests another dimension of the truth; for the door opens upon a certain limit. It offers access to the whole, but only in a certain way (*ti*), for we remain always incapable of part of it, never able to grasp the totality. Aristotle gestures to this incapacity with the little indefinite enclitic adjective, *ti,* perhaps the most important and indeed, playful, word of the Aristotelian corpus. It injects definitive statements with a dimension of uncertainty, a play of ambiguity, comic in its capacity to expose the pretense of au-

---

Hyland also recognizes the exposure of pretense as one dimension of the comic, see Drew A. Hyland, *Finitude and Transcendence in the Platonic Dialogues* (Albany: State University of New York, 1995), 128–37. For an account of the "Know Thyself" admonition that problematizes the "humility" interpretation embraced here, arguing that, for Socrates at least, the precept enjoins us to constitute the self in such a way that it can be guided by knowledge toward the good, see Christopher Moore, *Socrates and Self-Knowledge*, 1st edn. (Cambridge: Cambridge University Press, 2015).

28 *Meta.*, II.1, 993a30–993b7.

thority. The indefinite adverb serves in Aristotle throughout as a reminder of the tragicomic incapacity to grasp the whole, even as it affirms the attempt to enter the threshold that opens onto the appearance of things.

Aristotle's thinking lives largely along the limit of this threshold, advancing always into the possibility of that knowledge all humans desire,[29] yet returning ever again to the doorway, the liminal site of the perplexing ambiguity of appearing. This dynamic of advance and return can be heard in Aristotle's own articulation of the *pros hen* relation that orients his investigation into the meaning of being qua being. He begins at the threshold, advancing cautiously toward a principle capable of establishing a certain order without annihilating difference. He writes: "Being is said in many ways, but pointing toward one [*pros hen*] and some one nature [*mian tina phusin*] but not homonymously."[30] The approach is phenomenological: he attempts to attend to the many ways being is said in order to discern a certain one, a common nature to which they themselves point. Here the many ways being is said is heard to articulate something of the truth of being as plurivocal. For Aristotle, language is not a violence that closes access to the singular, but a natural phenomenon that opens us to the truth of things.

The truth of *pros hen* reference is heard in the way things are said. For example, a diversity of things are called healthy in reference to some one thing, namely, the healthy condition of an organic being. Thus, medicine is related to a healthy condition by restoring it, exercise by producing and maintaining it, the body by being receptive to it, and a ruddy complexion by being a sign of it. The many ways being is said point similarly to one source (*archē*), namely, substance, or *ousia*:

> For some things are called beings because they are *ousiai*, others because they are affections of *ousia*, some because they are ways into *ousia*, or destructions or deprivations or

---

29 *Meta.*, I.1, 980a21.
30 *Meta.*, IV.2, 1003a33–34.

qualities or the production or generation of *ousia*, or they are things said in relation to *ousia* or negations of any of these, on account of which it is even possible to say that nonbeing is not being.[31]

The assertive advance of *ousia* seems here unimpeded even by the strange appearance of nonbeing. This initial thrust appears to take on a comic hubris when it is heard along with that famous sentence at the beginning of the path of thinking that is the middle books of the *Metaphysics*: "And indeed, in earlier times and now and always the inquiry, indeed always the perplexity concerning what being is [*ti to on*] is just this: what is *ousia*?"[32] This shift from the perplexity concerning being (*to on*) to the concrete question "what is *ousia*?," when combined with the identification of *ousia* as the one nature toward which the investigation into being must be oriented, seems initially to reinforce Schürmann's insistence that *ousia* names the one hegemonic principle that sets all things in order.[33] However, to take this beginning of the inquiry into being as indicative of the overarching structure that reveals itself in the end is to fail to traverse the difficult path of thinking that leads to a dynamic apprehension of *ousia*, not as the product of manufacture, but as a living expression of living being. If Aristotle orients the investigation into being toward the one that is *ousia*, it will be necessary to hear the way in which this one is permitted to retain a certain singularity and is prevented from entering completely into the universal that would render it particular. Indeed, the introduction of *pros hen* reference was animated by Aristotle's

---

31 *Meta.*, IV.2, 1003b6–10.
32 *Meta.*, VII.1, 1028b1–3.
33 Schürmann puts it this way: "Substance is a principle of order: as the cause of accidents, it fulfills one and the same role in regard to them, that is, to maintain them in being; substance is furthermore part of their order since it functions as the first of the categories, and it transcends their order since they do not in turn cause it to be; it also orients and gives coherence to all predicaments; finally it founds an order that is not only logical but real, based on observation." See Schürmann, *Heidegger on Being and Acting*, 109.

recognition that being is not a universal genus, and so, if there was to be a single science of being, another way of thinking about the unifying nature of things would have to be delineated. *Pros hen* equivocation was initially designed to suggest a way to think being without subsuming the many ways of being under a single hegemonic universal principle.[34] It offers Aristotle a way of articulating the manner in which a diversity of phenomena enter into community with one another without sacrificing their unicity.

By orienting his investigation into being qua being toward the one nature that is *ousia,* Aristotle embarks upon a circuitous path of thinking that, however, complex, can be traced by attending briefly to two moments of turning in which the question, "what is *ousia*?" is itself transformed. The first moment of turning comes in chapter 17 of *Metaphysics* book VII, which Aristotle explicitly marks as an attempt to speak anew about *ousia* "as though making another beginning."[35] Here the original ontological question — "what is *ousia*?" — seems to have led to a series of impasses because it sought an answer in some concrete entity, rather than looking for that according to which each thing is one. Aristotle insists that *ousia* escapes notice "when the thing being sought is what is a human-being, because one states it simply and does not distinguish that these things are this thing [*hoti tade tode*]."[36] The new beginning Aristotle suggests involves, then, a shift in perspective that requires a transformation of the sort of question being asked. The what-question is no longer sufficient, instead, what must now be sought is "why the material is something." Aristotle continues, appealing first to an example from the region of fabrication, moving then to a living example, "so, 'why are these things [*tadi*] a house?', because the what it is for the house to be inheres. And this here [*todi*], or this

---

34 Joseph Owens has articulated the impetus behind Aristotle's introduction of the pros hen vocabulary along these lines. See Joseph Owens, *The Doctrine of Being in the Aristotelian Metaphysics,* vol. 3 (Toronto, Canada: Pontifical Institute of Mediaeval Studies, 1978), 269–75.
35 *Meta.,* VII.17 1041a6–7.
36 *Meta.,* VII.17, 1041a32–b2.

body [*to sōma touto*] holding itself this way, is a human-being. Thus, the cause of the matter is sought by which it is something, and this is the form [*eidos*]. But this is *ousia*."[37] This new beginning reveals the *eidos* as that which accounts for the matter's being held in a certain way such that it becomes whatever it is. This leads Aristotle to distinguish the material dimension of the individual from its form, calling the former an element and the later an *archē*, or principle.[38]

This shift from the what-question to the why-question, with its appeal to the example of the house, seems to reinforce Schürmann's insistence that Aristotle's conception of *ousia* fetishizes fabrication, reducing the inquiry into being to a search for causes that ends in the positing of the form as the ultimate principle of order. However, even as Aristotle attempts here to speak *ousia* anew, a proliferation of demonstratives — *tade, tode, touto* — anticipates yet another beginning, one oriented by yet a third kind of question. The demonstratives themselves demonstrate the extent to which Aristotle's thinking remains oriented to the being of concrete beings. The demonstratives literally point, again and again, to the site of ontological encounter that conditions the very appearing of *ousia*. Thus, the proliferation of demonstratives anticipates already the extent to which the causal account will need to give way to a more phenomenological orientation. Ousiology is not aetiology, but phenomenology.

The end of *Metaphysics* book VIII prepares the way for yet another beginning. There Aristotle translates the distinction between form and matter into the more dynamic vocabulary of *dunamis* and *energeia*, potency and being-at-work. He suggests that those who seek a cause of being in some thing beyond the being in question are misguided: "But as was said, the ultimate matter and the shape [*morphē*] are the same and one, the former as in potency, the later as being-at-work, so that seeking the cause of their being is like seeking what the cause of one thing is; for each is a certain one [*hen gar ti hekaston*], and that

---

37 *Meta.*, VII.17, 1041b4–9.
38 *Meta.*, VII.17, 1041b16–33.

which is in potency and that which is in activity are somehow one [*hen pōs estin*]."[39] The enclitic pronoun, *ti* — a "certain," and the enclitic adverb, *pōs* — "somehow," announce an indefiniteness at play in the being of the one. As potency and being-at-work, matter and form are each a *certain* one, nevertheless, they are together *somehow* one. An ambiguity of unicity emerges here that destabilizes *ousia*, forcing Aristotle to consider the perplexing question: *how* are these two one? The what-question gives way to the why-question, which now turns out to be the phenomenological question as to how *ousia* shows itself as one.

Aristotle pursues a response to this question in terms of *dunamis* and *energeia*, suggesting ultimately that these terms cannot be understood on the model of a conception of motion (*kinēsis*) bound up with the paradigm of production. In *Metaphysics* book IX, Aristotle delineates the difference between motions, like house building, that have their ends outside of themselves, and actions (*praxeis*), like living, that have their ends in themselves in order to suggest that the being of *ousia* is itself a *praxis* with its end in itself.[40] As such a *praxis*, *ousia* names a dynamic activity in which the being-at-work of a being does not relinquish its own potency-for-being. Such beings embody the living activity of possibility which Aristotle names *tode ti*, "this something," or "a certain this." Here the demonstrative *tode*, articulates the irreducible singularity of that which presents itself, while the indefinite *ti*, shatters the hermetic isolation of the singular, calling it into community with others. The *tode ti* expresses the individual as such. No longer singular, but not yet particular, the individual gives itself to articulation even as it retains something of an irreducible unicity.

Schürmann's account of hegemonic principles and the beginnings of metaphysics covers over the precariously situated individual that is the *tode ti*. The individual is eclipsed by the division of phenomena into irreducible singulars destined to be violated by the "brutal syntax" of a language that forces concepts

---

39 *Meta.*, VIII.6, 1045b17–21.
40 *Meta.*, IX.6, 1048b18–35.

upon them, and mere particulars, thoroughly dominated by the universals that rule over them.⁴¹ Yet, the dynamic poetics of Aristotle's thinking lingers on the site of the playful appearance of the individual, the beginner who lives as conditioned by its end. His thinking is able "to linger on the site in which we live"⁴² precisely because it refuses to deny the tragic limits that press in upon it, even as it attempts to articulate the truth that emerges there. It is no surprise, then, to find Schürmann encountering the poetics of Aristotelian thinking as he develops the distinction between natality and mortality in the initial stages of *Broken Hegemonies*.

The Play of Natality and Mortality:
The Appearing of the Individual

Let us begin again, then, by returning to the moment at which Schürmann articulates the ontological traits of natality and mortality. This distinction was said to remain caught in a metaphysical logic of dichotomy that prevents Schürmann from discerning the precariously situated individual who appears somehow between the anarchic singular and the subsumed particular. The metaphysical undertones of this dichotomy can be felt in the way it repeats the long tradition of privileging mortality, death and the tragic over natality, life and the comic. Yet in the same breath as Schürmann posits this dichotomy, he is careful to describe his project as testing the suspicion "that death joins life without, however, forming a tandem with it, that it does not reflect life symmetrically nor oppose it with a determinate negation."⁴³ Natality and mortality must be permitted to enter into an inherently unstable community, without the one being permitted to dominate the other and yet, without the two consolidating themselves into a stabilized whole. The moment Schürmann's thinking feels the pull of metaphysical theticism,

---

41 Schürmann, *Broken Hegemonies*, 19–20.
42 Cf. ibid., 3.
43 Ibid., 23.

the powerful subsumptive force of the one, it responds with a "dispersive counter-strategy"[44] that intentionally posits difference in an attempt to undermine the hegemonic authority of the principle of unity itself. Schürmann's is a thinking soberly bound to a ravaged site. "What if," writes Schürmann, "the common and the singular both bind us — then is it not rather that we inhabit a ravaged site?"[45]

Yet, to inhabit a ravaged site is to feel the tragic weight of singularity *along with* the comic desire for community. To be assiduously bound to such a site is to be ravaged *and* enrapt. It is to refuse to sacrifice the play of the comic upon the alter of the tragic; it is to hear in the call to community not only the annihilation of singularity, but also the allure of possibility, not merely the hegemonic operation of dominating principles, but also the injunction to inhabit a site, ravaged and enrapt, that opens a "network of potentials" within which justice first becomes possible.[46]

The very attempt to articulate the meaning of natality in its relation to mortality implicitly drives Schürmann back to the beginning of metaphysics to expose its duplicity. Turning again then to Aristotle, Schürmann hears more acutely the power of those little, playful words Aristotle deploys as signifiers of his own profound appreciation the ravaged site of enrapture that conditions his thinking. In referring again to the *pros hen* relation, Schürmann points to a passage in which the indefinite pronoun, *ti*, appears modifying the *pros hen* formulation itself, rendering it ambiguous, as if to undermine its capacity to consolidate at the very moment of its articulation.[47] Emphasizing

---

44 Ibid.
45 Ibid., 16.
46 Schürmann himself develops an understanding of responsibility along these lines at the end of the Heidegger book, using in that context the formulation "network of potentials." See Schürmann, *Heidegger on Being and Acting*, 263.
47 This passage reads: "For each being there is a leading-back toward a certain one (*pros hen ti*) and common thing..." and is found at *Meta*. XI.3, 1061a10–11. See also *Meta*. IV.2, 1003a33–34.

the significance of the indefinite, Schürmann says "the *ti* serves to muddle the concept, making it into an indirect description."[48] It seems, then, that language is capable not only of a violence that annihilates the singular, but also of a poetic response that does some justice to that remainder which does not enter completely into the concept, yet is nevertheless accessible to a poetic saying riveted to the ravaged site of rapture.

Thus, as always, there is more to that little word, *ti*, than it appears. For it marks the trace of an individuality Schürmann does not think even if his thinking opens the enigmatic space of its appearing. The *tode ti* is a poetic articulation of the individual as ravaged and enrapt. It is ravaged because bound on one side by the singularity it must relinquish to enter into community and on the other by the particularity that seeks to consume it. Yet, it is enrapt because exposed to a double bind that frees it for the possibility of connection within a rich and teeming "network of potentials." If, however, community is not to devolve ever and again into the politics of domination, the capacity to think, act, and live as conditioned by natality and mortality at once will need to be cultivated by habits of thinking and acting, indeed, by habits of speaking attuned to the poetic duplicity of beginnings. With the *tode ti* the political significance of the *pros hen* relation is transformed, for a thinking and acting directed toward such an insistently ambiguous one would need to operate with a heightened awareness of its own hegemonic tendencies; it would need to learn a certain poetics: the ability to respond to the duplicitous appearing of things in ways that do justice to duplicity and open new possibilities for community.

To begin to learn the habits of thinking and acting endemic to such a poetic politics, deeper and richer practices of beginning are needed. To that end, as morning gives way to afternoon, let us take up the question of incipience "as if making

---

48 Schürmann, *Broken Hegemonies*, 20. Schürmann goes on to suggest the Aristotle speaks often of *phusis tis*, which he translates as "something like a rising" in order to emphasize the extent to which Aristotle himself remains distant from that understanding of nature that serves as a supreme referent.

another beginning,"⁴⁹ and attend here to the final line from René Char's poem, the *Shark and the Gull,* a poem Schürmann himself translated into English:

> Make every supposed end be a new innocence, a feverish advance for those who stumble in the morning heaviness.⁵⁰

As the heaviness of morning "mounts into the eyes to crown the noon,"⁵¹ we begin again with Schürmann as he takes up a reading of Char's poem that leads us, oddly enough, to the heart of the work of Plotinus. Here we begin to discern a way to think natality and mortality together as we attempt to settle into the ravaged site of rapture where poetic politics first becomes possible.

---

49 *Meta.*, VII.17, 1041a6–7.
50 Reiner Schürmann, "Situating René Char: Hölderlin, Heidegger, Char and the 'There Is,'" *boundary 2* 4, no. 2 (January 1, 1976): 513–34, at 515.
51 Ibid.

*

Henri Matisse, "The Shark and the Gull"

"In May 1946 I sent the manuscript of the poem 'The Shark and the Gull' to Henri Matisse at Vence. During the visit that I had paid to the great painter we had not spoken of any poem in particular. I had convinced myself that Matisse was well and that his treasures continued being executed with the same sumptuous regularity as usual. Back at l'Isle-sur-Sorgue I sent him the manuscript of my poem (I love Matisse and his discrete goodness: this poem to thank him for a precise act). He answered me that in a recent series of drawings he had *discovered* the same theme. Here is one of these drawings."

René Char*

Le requin et la mouette

    Je vois enfin la mer dans sa triple harmonie, la mer qui tranche de son croissant la dynastie des douleurs absurdes, la grande volière sauvage, la mer crédule comme un liseron.

    Quand je dis: *j'ai levé la loi, j'ai franchi la morale, j'ai maillé le coeur,* ce n'est pas pour me donner raison devant ce pèse-néant dont la rumeur étend sa palme au delà de ma persuasion. Mais rien de ce qui m'a vu vivre et agir jusqu'ici n'est témoin alentour. Mon epaule peut bien sommeiller, ma jeunesse accourir. C'est de cela seul qu'il faut tirer richesse immédiate et opérante. Ainsi, il y a un jour de pur dans l'année, un jour qui creuse sa galerie merveilleuse dans l'écume de la mer, un jour qui monte aux yeux pour couronner midi. Hier la noblesse était déserte, le rameau etait distant de ses bourgeons. Le requin et la mouette ne communiquaient pas.

    O Vous, arc-en-ciel de ce rivage polisseur, approchez le navire de son espérance. Faites que toute fin supposée soit une neuve innocence, un fiévreux en avant pour ceux qui trebuchent dans la matinale lourdeur.[52]

---

[52] Schürmann, "Situating René Char," 515, cited from René Char, *Fureur et Mystère* (Paris: Gallimard, 1962), 197.

The Shark and the Gull

At last I see the triple harmony of the sea, whose crescent cuts the dynasty of absurd sufferings, the great wild aviary, the sea, credulous as a bindweed.

When I say: *I overcame the law, I transgressed morality, I unfurled the heart,* it is not to justify myself before this weigher of nothingness whose murmur extends its victory palm beyond my persuasion. But nothing that has seen me live and act hitherto is witness here. My shoulder may well sleep, my youth come running. From these alone immediate and operative riches must be drawn. Thus there is one day of purity in the year, a day that hollows its marvelous gallery into the sea-foam, a day that mounts into the eyes to crown the noon. Yesterday nobility was desert, the branch was distant from its swelling buds. The shark and the gull did not communicate.

Oh You, rainbow of this polishing shore, bring the ship closer to its hope. Make every supposed end be a new innocence, a feverish advance for those who stumble in the morning heaviness.[53]

---

53 Ibid. Translation by Schürmann.

3

Afternoon
Situating the Poetics of Politics

*Come, follow this way; follow
on your blind feet, father, where I lead you.*
  — Sophocles, *Oedipus Tyrannus, Antigone*, ll. 180–81[1]

In his 1976 translation and interpretation of René Char's poem, *The Shark and the Gull*, Reiner Schürmann gives voice to a sense of incipience that opens the possibility of a politics other than that founded upon archic domination. This other incipience is described as "nuptial," a signifier that appears momentarily in that essay, only to be indelibly, although almost indiscernibly, inscribed into the *tension* between the dual traits of natality and mortality that animates the topological analytic of ultimates in Schürmann's *Broken Hegemonies*. The symbol of the nuptial, which will be heard to give voice to the dynamic and asymmetrical union of natality and mortality, appears as Schürmann attempts to locate the origin of Char's poetry. This origin is situated in the poem itself, in the event of its articulation.[2] There a

---
1 Sophocles, *Sophoclis Fabulae* (Oxford: Clarendon Press, 1990).
2 Reiner Schürmann, "Situating René Char: Hölderlin, Heidegger, Char and the 'There Is,'" *boundary 2* 4, no. 2 (January 1, 1976): 513–34, at 518. For Schürmann, and for this chapter, to situate a text means to locate "the place from which it speaks" (518), that is, the *topos* of its *logos*. He writes: "To situate a script, that is, a way of writing determined by an understanding of be-

world begins, opened by and in a hermeneutical relation that brings to language an originary experience of the origin capable of transforming the meaning and nature of politics itself.[3]

Schürmann suggests the transformative power of the hermeneutical relation when he writes: "[T]o read is to interpret, to interpret is to exist in a new way. The hermeneutical relation concerns our reality, for the text interprets us."[4] Hermeneutics is transformative because it is rooted in what Schürmann calls "symbolic praxis." "Symbols," he writes, "effect the translation of discourse into a course, a path."[5] Symbols accomplish this translation by gathering discordant phenomena into relation in ways that point beyond themselves and enjoin a certain interpretive response. Symbolic gathering thus manifests a phenomenological difference — symbols show how phenomena withdraw as

---

ing, one has to give some thought to the locus out of which the poet speaks and writes…. To situate a work of prose or poetry is to raise the question of its beginning: where is the place from which the script originates?" (513).

3 Schürmann is always careful to articulate the many ways the origin is said and it is important here in the middle to attend to the difference between these ways of saying the beginning. In his Heidegger book, Schürmann writes: "The origin is said in many ways: the metaphysical *archai* and *principia*, and phenomenological 'original' and 'originary' — the original rise of a mode of being (*Seiendheit*, beingness) and the originary rise which is the event of being." Reiner Schürmann, *Heidegger on Being and Acting: From Principles to Anarchy* (Bloomington: Indiana University Press, 1987), 151. The nuptial, as will be heard, articulates the originary as opposed to the original: "The *original* modes of appearing are countless; they are as numerous as the disjunctive moments in history. The *originary* mode of appearing, on the other hand, has no history." The nuptial *describes* the originary origin: "The originary origin, 'the rise that presences at the same time as it withdraws into itself,' is always implicated in what we live and understand. But it is rarely grasped for its own sake." See ibid., 140. The nuptial speaks the originary origin for its own sake, though of course, without grasping it conceptually. The political importance of the nuptial will be discernible in the way it poetically articulates a community rooted in a union that appears as an event of originary presencing.

4 Reiner Schürmann, "Symbolic Difference," *The Graduate Faculty Philosophy Journal* 19/20, no. 2/1 (1997): 28.

5 Ibid., 33.

they enter into constellation.⁶ In so doing, symbols undermine every attempt to impose a univocal order of meaning upon the gathering of phenomena into community. The political significance of symbols can thus be felt in the way the phenomenological difference they bring to expression enjoins a response other than that of archic domination. By awakening us to the originary duplicity of appearing, symbols set us on a path of response capable of transforming existing realities and opening us to new possibilities of relation.⁷ Schürmann thematizes symbolic praxis and the response it invites in terms of a certain *poietics*:

> The phenomenology of the symbol gives one food for thought: it is speculative insofar as it reflects the origin which shows itself while it hides. The *poietics* of the symbol give one something to do. Symbols create. The praxis which they invite us to is not inaugurated by man, but by the symbols themselves.⁸

---

6   Ibid., 15. There Schürmann insists that to which the symbol refers "manifests and hides itself at the same time."
7   Schürmann thus refers also to a "symbolic difference" which he is careful to distinguish from the "ontological difference." This latter refers, of course, to Heidegger's insistence on a distinction between "'being' as the 'being of being' and 'being' as 'being' with regard to its own proper sense, that is, with regard to its truth (clearing)." See Martin Heidegger, *Unterwegs zur Sprache* (Frankfurt am Main: Vittorio Klosterman, 1985), 110. Schürmann suggests that if the ontological difference gives being to be thought, the symbolic difference gives "being to be thought, insofar as it calls man onto his originary path. The symbolic difference is not thought in the service of man, any more than the ontological difference. But it says more than the ontological difference: it states the itinerant-wandering which being inflicts on existence awakened to symbols." See Schürmann, "Symbolic Difference," 34. Thus, symbolic difference points already to a kind of praxis that emerges as a response to phenomenological difference.
8   Reiner Schürmann, "Symbolic Praxis," *The Graduate Faculty Philosophy Journal* 19/20, no. 2/1 (1997): 39–65, at 39–40. Schürmann writes "poietics," it seems, to gesture to the duplicity of the Greek *poiēsis* discussed in chapter 2. See Schürmann, *Heidegger on Being and Acting*, 136 and 303. In speaking of a "poetics of politics" rather than a "poietics of politics," we do not deny the duplicity of *poiēsis*. However, to speak of a "poetics" is at once to emphasize the creative openness endemic to symbolic praxis and to insist that the

Symbolic praxis, then, involves an invitation to action communicated to human-beings awake to the duplicitous gathering of symbols. As symbolic, it is a praxis rooted in ambiguity and yet held accountable to the play of appearing articulated by and in the symbol itself. To enter into dialogue with the symbol is to be mobilized by a praxis that is other than the politics of domination which seeks to consolidate authority under a univocal order of meaning, a politics bound ineluctably to the tragic denial endemic to all thetic legislation.[9]

Perhaps, then, a dialogue with the symbol of the nuptial as it announces itself in Schürmann's reading of *The Shark and the Gull* will itself set us on a path toward another politics. This other politics would be poetic insofar as it opens us to new possibilities of relation rooted in a responsive attunement to the happening of truth in the gathering of community.

Situating the Nuptial

The symbol of the nuptial announces itself in an essay that appears in 1976, the year Schürmann also published "Le praxis

---

productive side of poiesis must ultimately be held accountable to that which eludes the techniques of fabrication.

9 In this, Schürmann's symbolic praxis resonates with and anticipates the poetry of Jeroen Mettes. In his essay "Political Poetry: A Few Notes. Poetics for N30," Mettes articulates the meaning of poetic politics in its connection with symbolic practice: "A poem does something," he writes, "[w]here there is a sentence, there is always a world." The capacity for a poem to "do something" is rooted in the creative capacity of its symbols and the world opened through its sentences. Mettes further develops this as he considers the political poetry, which he calls "pure poetry." "Political poetry means: a poetry that dares to think about itself, about its language and about its world and about the problematic relation between both, which is this relation as problem. A poetry that thinks at all, articulates its problem. ... It is no rational engagement, but an aversion against everything that obstructs life, and love for everything what is worthy of having been loved. The world is engaged with me, not the other way around." See Jeroen Mettes, "Political Poetry: A Few Notes. Poetics for N30," trans. Vincent W.J. van Gerven Oei, *continent*. 2, no. 1 (2012): 29 and 35, http://continentcontinent.cc/index.php/continent/article/view/80.

symbolique."[10] As a symbol, the nuptial gathers by pointing beyond itself to a sense of inception other than the epochal beginning Schürmann identifies with the trait of natality in his last published work, *Broken Hegemonies*. There, natality is most often bound to a logic of thetic maximization that forces phenomena into concepts, traces causes to ultimate conditions, and subsumes singulars under universals that render them docile and particular.[11] If natality asserts the politics of hegemony and repression, nuptiality announces the poetic politics of symbolic praxis that remains attuned to and held accountable by the duplicity of beginning which shows itself each time beings enter into relation with one another.

To discern the contours of the poetics of politics opened by the symbol of the nuptial, it will be decisive to attend carefully, albeit briefly, to the situation from which an articulation of the nuptial itself arises; for the phenomenological meaning of the term should neither be confused nor conflated with the traditional practices of marriage and the legislation under which they operate. The "nuptial" appears in hermeneutical relation to Char's poem, which itself begins by lending voice to a certain gathering of community by attending to the sea as it enters into constellation with the sky: "At last I see the triple harmony of the sea, whose crescent cuts the dynasty of absurd sufferings, the great wild aviary, the sea, credulous as a bindweed."[12] The arc of this crescent, which Schürmann suggests "traces a bulging line like a women before childbirth" and thus, we might add, points already to a union more originary than natality, unites

---

10 The essay on symbolic praxis cited above was originally published in French as Reiner Schürmann, "Le praxis symbolique," *Cahiers Internationaux de Symbolisme* 29–30 (1976): 145–70.
11 See Reiner Schürmann, *Broken Hegemonies*, trans. Reginald Lilly (Bloomington: Indiana University Press, 2003), 18–19. This is but one of a number of sites in *Broken Hegemonies* in which natality is associated with an understanding of *archē* that "designates to us the attribute of some being that dominates" (158) or "attaches itself absolutely to one representation, relativizing all others, and conferring upon it a hyperbolic prestige" (279) or "bears us toward the figures of the common" (528).
12 Schürmann, "Situating René Char," 515.

the sky and the sea. For Schürmann, the key to the poem is the manner in which it aspires, in its very articulation, to unite the various oppositions that appear in its symbolic imagery. The very title, *The Shark and the Gull,* gestures at once to these oppositions — between the horizontal and vertical, duration and instant, weight and levity, sea and sky — and to their unity. Yet the world in which these oppositions communicate is opened only in dialogue with the poem itself. Schürmann puts it this way: "[W]hen the poem is said and understood, the world just begins. But its world lasts as briefly as the poem itself."[13] This poetic world is thus always already disappearing, its natality is mortal; and yet its mortality, in opening new possibilities of relation, is itself natal.

The nuptial articulates the discordant union of mortal natality and natal mortality that appears as a world opens in dialogue with the poem. Schürmann introduces the "nuptial" as he traces the way the poem brings this union to language as an event of originary presencing.[14] This is what he says:

> Two notions of the origin appear to be phenomenologically defensible: the origin as the presence of what is present, and the origin as cause. The first may be described as nuptial: Char's poem announces the nuptials of the shark and the gull. The second may be called natal: cosmogonies speak of the cause or nascency of the world. Both notions imply an

---

13 Ibid., 518.
14 The nuptial is a recurring trope in Char's poetry. See, for example, *Le Visage nuptial* in *Fureur et mystère* and *Rougeur des matinaux* in *Les Matinaux.* See René Char, *The Dawn Breakers/Les Matinaux* (Newcastle on Tyne: Bloodaxe Books, 1992). A powerful articulation of the event of presencing can be heard in a collection entitled Recheche de la base et du sommet: "that instant when beauty, so long awaited, rises out of common things, crosses our radiant field of vision, binds together all that can be bound, lights all that must be lit in our shear of shadows." Cited and translated in Nancy Kline Piore, *Lightning: The Poetry of René Char* (Boston: Northeastern University Press, 1981), xviii.

event, but nuptials occur in the present whereas nascency is a happening of the past, of the beginning of an era.¹⁵

The poetic origin is "nuptial" insofar as it expresses phenomenologically the event of union as a gathering that remains attuned and responsive to the presencing of what is present. The epochal origin is, on the other hand, "natal" in the sense that it predicates a beginning of the past so as to institute and legitimize an era of archic sovereignty.¹⁶

Schürmann's own attempt in *Broken Hegemonies* to trace the thetic fantasms that have historically installed themselves, ruled and withered within each era of archic sovereignty remains so intimately attentive to the unfolding of epochal origins that it fails to appropriately articulate the political possibilities endemic to the poetic origin its own analytic so poignantly brings to language. Animated by a logic of ultimates in which the natal and the mortal emerge as the two decisive phenomenological traits that mark the topology of western epochal history, *Broken Hegemonies* speaks more of the tragic discord between natality and mortality than it does of the dynamic tension that is their poetic union. This emphasis on discord is rooted its the rigorous attempt to trace the diremption that "signifies the loss of every hegemony."¹⁷ Diremption here is distinguished from the mere destitution that describes what happens to a hegemonic principle when it loses its force of law. Epochal history is marked

---

15 Schürmann, "Situating René Char," 519.
16 Emanuela Bianchi distinguishes between Schürmann's and Arendt's understanding of natality this way: "For Schürmann, natality indicates from the start a subsumption in commonality, whereas for Arendt it indicates the arising of what is singular and extraneous to what is already established." See Emanuela Bianchi, "Natal Bodies, Mortal Bodies, Sexual Bodies: Reading Gender, Desire, and Kinship through Reiner Schürmann's *Broken Hegemonies*," *Graduate Faculty Philosophy Journal* 33, no. 1 (April 1, 2012): 57–84 58. Here, then, the nuptial might be recognized as announcing a natality that points to commonality without being subsumptive. Because the nuptial refuses all economies of subsumption, it is perhaps better able to do justice to the emergence of the singular to which Arendtian natality points.
17 Schürmann, *Broken Hegemonies*, 623.

by the destitution of one hegemonic principle as it gives rise to the re-institution of another. Diremption, on the other hand, means "first of all an expiration has happened, the annihilation of normative acts that cleanses the tragic condition."[18] *Broken Hegemonies* repeatedly insists upon the discordant relation between natality and mortality in order to give poignant voice to the destructive logic of all thetic acts, indeed, to the *diremption* of normative consciousness that brings epochal history to an end.[19]

If, however, in *Broken Hegemonies* a tendency to maximize natality comes to mute the nuptial, it is precisely the rigorous phenomenological articulation of the logic proper to broken epochal hegemonies that allows the nuptial to come to language in the text itself. As Char puts it in his poem, *Redness of the Dawnbreakers*: "If you destroy, then may it be with nuptial tools."[20] Perhaps *Broken Hegemonies* may be heard to destroy with nuptial tools. Indeed, in the text itself we hear something of what Schürmann discerns in *The Shark and the Gull*:

> In or with the poem the world begins. Char's language is originary in the sense that it is itself the origin of what the poem achieves. We take the word "origin" literally: *oriri*, to rise, to appear, to come forth. Thus we say that language here gives rise to poetry which in turn gives rise to a world unified.[21]

In speaking of a "world unified" by and in poetic saying, Schürmann opens the possibility of thinking politics as rooted in a poetics capable of gathering the discordant into community

---

18 Ibid., 514. Later, Schürmann explicitly draws the meaning of diremption [*dessaisie*] into contrast with "the heart of the grip [*saisie*] making up the epoch" (529). It is necessary, therefore, to think diremption in Schürmann in terms other than the conceptual, which must be said to grasp, *saisir,* or in German, *greifen,* that which it seeks to capture. Diremption announces the expiration of a mode of understanding that seizes.
19 Schürmann locates the phenomenon of diremption ultimately in the thinking of Martin Heidegger and specifically in Heidegger's *Beiträge zur Philosophie.* See ibid., 529.
20 Char, *The Dawn Breakers/Les Matinaux,* 151.
21 Schürmann, "Situating René Char," 518.

without colluding in the consolidation of authority by denying the differend.[22] Indeed, Schürmann's own text, *Broken Hegemonies,* is originary in the sense that it is itself the origin of the poetic politics achieved in and through its very articulation. Where Char's poem *says:* "The shark and gull did not communicate," Schürmann's text *says:* "Natality and mortality ... are ultimates in differend."[23] Yet, Schürmann's hermeneutical dialogue with Char's poem opens a world in which the shark and gull do communicate:

> In the now of the poem the shark and the gull do communicate at last. The gull is constant leaving, vertical flight, whereas the shark settles in the depth, gravity is its shelter. The gull has no refuge. When both communicate, the rainbow appears, offspring of the light and water drops. The sky and the ocean mingle. The poem aspires to the union of the two opposite dimensions down to the prayer that concludes it.[24]

So too might we enter into dialogue with Schürmann's text in such a way that mortality and natality do communicate at last. Mortality is constant dispersion, the counter-thrust of sin-

---

[22] As discussed in chapter one, a subtle but decisive distinction needs to be heard between the "differend" and "discordance." To reiterate: Throughout *Broken Hegemonies,* Schürmann appeals to the differend to speak of an order disturbed, of a conflict endemic to legislation "between the thesis of the same and a non-thetic other." See Schürmann, *Broken Hegemonies,* 32. Discord, on the other hand, names the incongruous manner in which life joins with death without consolidating under a common authority. In speaking of the incongruity that joins death to life, Schürmann clarifies the difference between the differend and discordance. To cite the relevant passage again: "Strictly speaking, the undertow it [death] exerts no longer gives rise to a differend, but to a discordance — if at least by differend one understand[s] the conflict of disparate laws calling for an impossible common authority. I speak of a differend only to describe this call and the referents that are posited to fulfill it in an illusory manner." Ibid., 551. For a discussion of the differend in Schürmann, see chapter four, below.

[23] For Char, see Schürmann, "Situating René Char," 515. For Schürmann, see Schürmann, *Broken Hegemonies,* 628.

[24] Schürmann, "Situating René Char," 518. The prayer that concludes the poem is the passage that concludes the last chapter, an end that points to a beginning that charts a path rather than imposes an order.

gularity, whereas natality settles into language, the common is its shelter. When both communicate, the nuptial appears, opening a space of symbolic praxis held at once accountable to the duplicity of originary incipience where the swell of natality joins with the undertow of a singularizing finitude. The text aspires to the union of these two discordant traits down to the suspicion it is said to test:

> [T]hat the other of life does not fit in well with it; that their discord has always been known to us, however confusedly; that death joins life without, however, forming a tandem with it, that it does not reflect life symmetrically nor oppose it with a determinate negation.[25]

Yet this suspicion is articulated in a profusion of negations that cover over the discordant union toward which it points. So long as this union designates a relation rooted in domination, its articulation must revert to the sort of apophatic saying that has "traditionally served the interests of maximization."[26] Here, however, the apophatic manner in which the suspicion that animates *Broken Hegemonies* is articulated gestures to a discordant otherness that eludes the economy of hegemonic domination. What is here said in an apophatic voice points already to an *apophantic* saying capable of articulating phenomena as they show themselves to be.[27] No world is opened by apophatic negation. Only the audacity to speak cataphatically has the power to bring to language the poetic presencing that is the event of union.[28]

---

25 Schürmann, *Broken Hegemonies*, 23.
26 Ibid., 149. For Schürmann, negative theology, which deploys apophatic speech, is driven ultimately by an attempt to gesture to an ultimate authority that is able to set the world in order without being subjected to the dominion it institutes.
27 For a discussion of this sense of apophantic saying, see chapter four, below and Christopher P. Long, *Aristotle on the Nature of Truth* (New York: Cambridge University Press, 2011), 96–115.
28 In his lectures on Plotinus at the New School during the fall semester of 1992, Schürmann associated the cataphatic in Plotinus with experience and the apophatic with language and conceptual thought. There he insisted that

Cataphatic saying, however, if it is not to succumb to its own maximizing tendencies, must endeavor to become apophantic by tempering its audacity with gentleness. The gentle audacity of apophantic saying involves a symbolic praxis that sets us on a path toward the poetics of politics by remaining attuned to and held accountable by the nuptial union of natality and mortality that opens whenever phenomena enter into constellation.

Schürmann's hermeneutical engagement with Char's poem is marked by precisely such a gentle audacity: it audaciously speaks the nuptial by attending carefully and responding caringly to what the poem says. The symbol of the nuptial that emerges here opens an originary encounter with the origin that directs us toward a poetics of politics. This path leads, however, in a rather surprising direction, for the nuptial comes to language most poignantly in the gentle but audacious reading of Plotinus Schürmann undertakes in *Broken Hegemonies*. In Plotinus, Schürmann locates an articulation of the one as *hēnosis*, the event of originary uniting that "takes place wherever beings enter into a constellation."[29] More specifically, Schürmann hears in the bold and enigmatic Plotinian treatise on *The Freedom and the Will of the One*, an articulation of "union not just as *epekeina*, going beyond beingness, but also as *hapax*, occurring in an event."[30] In Schürmann's own attempt to read this event of union in Plotinus, we hear an expression of the discordant union of natality and mortality that can more aptly be described as "nuptial." To further situate the poetics of politics, then, it will be

---

experience goes further than thought. However, by introducing the notion of *apophantic* saying here, a way of saying is opened that, as Adorno might say, does not go into conceptual thinking without remainder. See Theodor W. Adorno, *Negative Dialectics*, trans. E.B. Ashton (New York: Continuum, 1994), 5.

29 Schürmann, *Broken Hegemonies*, 147. References to the one in Plotinus are not marked by a capital "O" in order to emphasize that the one is no hypostasis in Plotinus, nor can it be hypostasized. The gesture is meant to unsettle the tendency to think the one as the ultimate cause or most authoritative substance at the foundation of a metaphysical system.

30 Ibid.

necessary to follow the trace the nuptial as it comes to language in Schürmann's audacious reading of Plotinus.

The Supposed End

Initially, Plotinus is said to mark the end of the Greek epoch. He speaks, Schürmann says, "for the destitution of the *hen-fantasm*."[31] Yet already at the beginning one hears in Schürmann's voice another possibility; for he qualifies this initial claim by saying "for the moment" Plotinus must be heard to speak on behalf of the end of the hegemony of the one. Further, in justifying his appeal to Plotinus as the site of the destitution of the Greek epoch, Schürmann rejects the possibility that Proclus, who appears two centuries after Plotinus, ought to be considered the last Greek philosopher. Rather, for Schürmann, "Plotinus *began anew*. Neoplatonism means, with him at least, a new Platonism. In Plotinus, we have a creative recommencement that more truly marks an ending than does the learned recapitulation of a Proclus."[32] Plotinus articulates an end precisely because his thinking is audaciously new. Yet his thinking is not simply a creative recommencement that marks the end in the sense of the destitution of one archic principle that gives rise to the institution of another. Rather, already in Plotinus a diremption can be heard, one that announces the expiration of a certain normative strategy, however ubiquitous and influential that strategy has historically been since the appearance of Plotinus himself. Although he continues to think of Plotinus as marking the destitution of the *hen*-fantasm, the way he reads Plotinus as anticipating Heidegger implicitly suggests that something like a diremption might be at stake:

> The debt [to Heidegger] is greater here than in any other of the readings in which I will try to arouse the poignancy of the "legislating tragic." Summoning the law before the letter of

---

31 Ibid., 139.
32 Ibid.

the *Enneads* would indeed not have been thinkable without anticipating — if only as a simple reading tool, displaced over seventeen centuries to foreign surroundings — the *occurrent singularization* in which one will recognize, at the end of the journey with Heidegger, the contretemps of mortality which has always broken hegemonies.[33]

Yet perhaps this "simple reading tool" is itself the "nuptial tool" by which Schürmann, in reading Plotinus, opens a way to think the natal and mortal together. By anticipating the diremption of the epochal history of metaphysical theticism to come, Schürmann is able to hear in Plotinus another beginning, one that, despite Schürmann's own insistence on destitution, does not of necessity give rise to yet another economy of archic domination. With Plotinus, the supposed end appears as a new innocence.

The New Innocence

Schürmann gives voice to this new innocence as he enters into dialogue with *Ennead* III.7 [45], *On Eternity and Time*.[34] There he hears an expression of "pure natality" that shows itself along a path of thinking Plotinus undertakes but abandons too soon. The direction of the thinking of III.7 is striking. Rather than beginning with time in order to discern something of eternity, Plotinus begins directly with an experience of eternity itself. Thus Plotinus writes:

---

33 Ibid., 140.
34 References to the texts of Plotinus will follow the convention in which roman numerals designate the *Ennead*, followed by a period and a number referring to the tractate of the *Ennead*. The number corresponding to Porphyry's chronological ordering of the texts is then placed in square brackets. Finally, the chapter and the line numbers follow, separated by commas. Translations are my own but remain informed by: Plotinus, A.H. Armstrong, and Porphyry, *Plotinus* (Cambridge: Harvard University Press, 1966). Because Schürmann himself admired the beautifully literary, if not always literally accurate, translations of MacKenna, these too have been consulted and, where particularly poignant, drawn upon. See Stephen MacKenna, *Plotinus: The Enneads* (London: Penguin Books, 1991).

> And at first we enquire concerning eternity, what sort of thing those who posit it as different from time consider it to be; for when we know that which stands as a paradigm, it will perhaps become clear how it is with the image, which they say that time is.³⁵

In approaching the question of time along the descending path from paradigm to image, Plotinus reverses the path pursued in the *Timeaus*.³⁶ For Schürmann this descending path is of decisive importance in the treatise on time because it invites us to think, without itself explicitly articulating, the temporality of the one itself. Schürmann insists that although the attempt to think the originary temporality of the one raises "the most arduous question — heretical within the Neoplatonic tradition," it can be heard nevertheless in the phenomenological difference that emerges as Plotinus seeks to articulate the way eternity

---

35 *En.* III.7 [45], 1, 17–19.
36 The *Timeaus* begins with an account of the motion endemic to the corporeal universe and the soul in order to identify time first as a copy of the eternal before undertaking a consideration of the paradigm itself. See Plato, *Platonis Opera* (New York: Oxford University Press, 1995), *Timeaus*, 36d8–37d1. Insofar as Plotinus pursues the nature of time beginning with eternity and the Intelligence, his path differs from that of Aristotle as well, who seeks the nature of time in the order of motion and links it closely with the soul. See Aristotle, *Aristotelis Physica* (Oxford: Oxford University Press, 1992), 218b9ff and 223a16ff. As Manchester points out, Plotinus's account of time, whatever its innovations, remains bound to a Platonic tradition that treats time and eternity as a single problematic. In this regard, Aristotle and the Stoics, who treat time independently of eternity, are the exceptions. See Peter Manchester, "Time and the Soul in Plotinus, III 7 (45), 11," *Dionysius* 2 (1978): 101–36, at 134. Even so, there remains a way in which Plotinus's method resonates with Aristotle's, for Aristotle begins, strictly speaking, not with the order of motion, but with the things said by his predecessors and with popular belief (217b29–218b9), while Plotinus too is concerned to save the things said by those who came before. For a discussion of the importance of Aristotle's methodological approach that begins by attending to the things said, see Christopher P. Long, "Saving *Ta Legomena*: Aristotle and the History of Philosophy," *The Review of Metaphysics* 60, no. 2 (2006): 247–67. This article was the core of chapter three of Long, *Aristotle on the Nature of Truth*.

unfolds as time.[37] By attending carefully to what Plotinus says about the temporality that marks the relation between the hypostatic Intelligence and the hypostatic Soul, Schürmann seeks to say something audacious about the originary temporality of the one.

As Plotinus articulates the manner in which eternity appears, a difference between the everlasting and the eternal announces itself. This difference is experienced as the soul turns directly toward the eternal, theorizing it intently. Thus, Plotinus says:

> What then, if one should not in any way depart from one's theorizing of it, but would be joined with it [*sunōn*], wondering at its very nature and able to act this way by an unwavering nature? One would oneself be moving toward eternity and never falling away from it at all, in order to be like [*homoios*] it and eternal [*aiōnion*], theorizing [*theōmenos*] eternity [*ton aiōna*] and the eternal [*to aiōnios*] by the eternal [*aiōnion*] in oneself."[38]

The very act of theorizing, which comes here to expression in the middle voice of the present participle, *theōmenos*, quite literally articulates the dynamic and ongoing participation of the soul in the eternal toward which it is directed.[39] The sort of participation this participle expresses, however, is not the traditional Platonic conception of participation which operates according to a logic of subsumption by which singulars are rendered particular as they are comprehended by the universal. Rather, the soul participates in the eternal by virtue of a joining that preserves difference in community. Schürmann would call this sort of joining "singular union," which comes to language in the middle voice and is distinguished from "transitive particu-

---

37 Schürmann, *Broken Hegemonies*, 151.
38 *En.* III.7 [45], 5, 9–12.
39 The ongoing dimension of this participation is heard in the progressive-repeated aspect endemic to the Greek present tense of the participle *theōmenos*. It is reinforced by the appeal to an unwavering nature that seems to belong to the soul itself.

larization," which operates by subsumption.⁴⁰ The voice of the participle itself expresses an event of discordant union that can best be described as *nuptial*.

Although in *Broken Hegemonies* Schürmann does not speak of the *nuptial*, it comes nevertheless to language as he traces the manner in which eternity appears in Plotinus. The activity of theorizing affords the soul direct access to the eternal and enables it to follow along the deductive path that follows eternity as it moved without compelling the soul to begin with time in search of its causal origin. Thus, Plotinus begins by attending to a nuptial union that is always already accessible to the soul: the union to which the soul is awoken as it turns its theorizing toward the eternal in itself and thus to eternity itself.⁴¹ This theorizing accomplishes a return to the higher level hypostatic Intelligence. It opens a phenomenological approach to eternity that involves experiential description, in cataphatic language that thus becomes apophantic, of the self-manifesting of eternity. This description gives voice to the phenomenological difference between eternity and everlastingness. Schürmann attends to this difference in an attempt to think the enigmatic temporality of the one.

Listen, first, to Plotinus's description:

---

40 Schürmann, *Broken Hegemonies*, 150–51. Schürmann does not develop the idea of singular union in reference to the specific participle, *theōmenos*, heard here in III.7 [45], 5, 12. However, the appearance of the middle-voiced participle in this context beautifully amplifies Schürmann's reading.

41 Plotinus famously describes the manner in which the soul joins the Intelligence as an awakening: "Many times I have woken into myself from the body, I come to be outside other things and inside myself." IV.8 [6], 1,1–3. Hadot uses the more modern, though perhaps not anachronisitic, vocabulary of the unconscious and consciousness. See Pierre Hadot, *Plotinus or The Simplicity of Vision* (Chicago: University of Chicago Press, 1993), 25. The turn inward to the self is for Plotinus also always a return upward toward the Intelligence and the one — a return that is accomplished by theorizing. See, for example, *En.* III.8 [30], 8, 1ff and *En.* IV.8 [6], 4, 1–4 and 28–33. Plotinus also describes the activity of the one itself as "something like being awake" (*En.* VI.8 [39], 16, 30ff).

If, then, what holds itself thusly [theorizing], is eternal [*aiōnion*] and always existing [*aei on*], that which does not in any respect fall away into another nature, having life, which it already has as a whole, not having received [*proslabon*] any addition, nor receiving any [*proslambanon*], nor about to receive any [*proslēpsomenon*], then that which holds thusly would be everlasting [*aidion*]; and everlastingness [*aidiotēs*] would be this sort of settled condition of the substrate, existing from and in it, but eternity [*aiōn*] would be the substrate with this sort of settled condition manifesting itself [*emphainomenēs*].[42]

This passage gives voice to a difference between everlastingness (*aidiotēs*) and eternity (*aiōn*).[43] Everlastingness is the self-manifesting of eternity. It expresses the eternal as it proceeds from hypostatic Intelligence to Soul. The peculiar dynamics of this appearing is articulated again in the middle voice, here with the present participle: *emphainomenēs*. If the progressive aspect of this word expresses the ongoing nature of everlastingness itself, its middle voice brings to language the singular union that marks the very appearing of eternity.[44] Eternity names the

---

[42] *En.* III.7 [45], 5, 12–18. Note how Plotinus gives voice to the temporality relinquished by this sort of theorizing as he varies the tenses of three participles of the same verb, *lambanein*, to receive: the aorist, *proslabon*, the present, *proslambanon*, and the future, *prolēpsomenon*. Each tense expresses an ecstasy of time collapsed into pure presence as the Soul theorizes the eternal. This shows the extent to which Plotinus was attuned to the philosophical significance of the way things are said. The tenses themselves show the temporal difference between eternity and time. For another, somewhat different example of how things said touch upon the truth, see *En.* V.5 [32], 5, 14–22.

[43] Jonas articulates a threefold difference in German between "Ewig-heit" (everlastingness, *aidiotēs*), "das Ewige" (the eternal, *aiōnion*), and "Ewigkeit" (eternity, *aiōn*). See Hans Jonas, "Plotin über Ewigkeit und Zeit," in *Politische Ordnung und menschliche Existenz: Festgabe für Eric Voegelin zum 60. Geburtstag* (Munich: Verlag C.H. Beck, 1962), 303.

[44] The genitive here resonates with the middle voice of the participle insofar as it remains ambiguously situated between the subjective and objective in a way that dissolves their strict opposition and thus allows, perhaps, the

temporality of the hypostatic Intelligence itself. Jonas puts it this way: "Eternity [*Ewigkeit*] is thus a substantial concept and designates not only a way of being, but rather the real realm of being which is real in this way" — that is, the hypostatic Intelligence.[45]

If, however, everlastingness emerges as the Soul turns (*epistrophē*) towards Intelligence, "theorizing eternity [*ton aiōna*] and the eternal [*to aiōnios*] by the eternal [*aiōnion*] in oneself," it cannot be understood as a copy of eternity, for as Plotinus explicitly says, everlastingness is "a settled condition of the substrate, existing from and in it." Everlastingness belongs to eternity itself.[46] Thus, eternity is described as a substrate with everlastingness manifesting itself. Eternity discloses itself as ev-

---

hegemonic logic of their dichotomy to expire. The translation "manifesting itself" is an inadequate attempt to articulate the middle voice in English. Schürmann insists on the inadequacy of using reflexivity to express the middle voice which must be heard to articulate the event in discord with itself. Schürmann writes: "It is the event enunciated in the middle voice, which is to say, one with neither agent nor patient. Modern languages render it with the reflexive. *Phuesthai* is translated as 'to raise *itself*,' *phainesthai* as 'to show *itself*.' However the middle voice does not thematize reflexivity any more than transitivity does. It does not express any operation of a subject on an object, or of a subject on itself. It does not give terms to thought." See Schürmann, *Broken Hegemonies*, 38.

45 See Jonas, "Plotin über Ewigkeit und Zeit," 303.

46 Beierwaltes puts it this way, endorsing Jonas's distinction between *Ewigheit* and *Ewigkeit*: "So it can be said that *aiōn* and *aidiotēs* are different names for the same thing from different perspectives. Herein the analogy touches upon the question concerning the identity of *nous* and *aiōn*. — The distinction [Jonas makes] between '*Ewigheit*' and '*Ewigkeit*' meets the mark of Plotinian thinking." See Werner Beierwaltes, *Über Ewigkeit und Zeit (Enneade III 7)* (Frankfurt am Main: Vittorio Klosterman, 1995), 156. Beierwaltes also suggests that Jonas undermines his own distinction by refusing to recognize a distinction between *aidios* and *aiōnios* at *En*. III.7 [45], 3, 2. See Jonas, "Plotin über Ewigkeit und Zeit", 297n3. Even if Plotinus does not yet articulate a difference between *aidios* and *aiōnios* in III.7 [45], 3, 2, by the time he suggests that the soul must theorize *ton aiōna* and *to aiōnios* by *to aiōnion* in oneself, a subtle difference between *aiōnios* and *aiōn* seems to have appeared, one that presses the *aiōnion* decisively in the direction of the *aidios* insofar as it seems to designate the way eternity (*aion*) is "in oneself" and indeed, the way one can be "like" (*homoios*) eternity (see, III.7 [45], 5, 11–12). Thus, already at the beginning of the passage that leads to the phenomenological difference between everlastingness and eternity, Plotinus seems to

erlastingness, an appearing that alters eternity as if by concealing it. Schürmann puts it this way: "In appearing, eternity both manifests and conceals itself."[47]

The dynamics of appearing, however, only reveal themselves as Plotinus attempts to describe the procession of eternity, a description made possible by the nuptial union accomplished by a theorizing turned assiduously toward eternity itself. Even so, however, eternity never appears in its pure presence. To discern eternity in its full presence would require recourse to the hypostasis above it, but there is no such, for eternity is "the life, always the same, of real being around the one" and the one is, strictly speaking, no hypostasis at all.[48] This is because the one has no higher level toward which to turn in an act of hypostatic founding. The one announces the expiration of foundational metaphysics.[49] As Jonas has beautifully suggested, the Plotinian speculative system, like those of a diverse group of other thinkers at the time, required that each hypostasis establish itself by a "two-beat rhythm" which involves not only the downward procession but also a reversal of direction and upward movement, a *proodos* and *epistrophē*.[50] As Jonas puts it, "precisely this double movement is the complete act of its [the hypostasis's] foundation."[51] This two-beat movement of foundation is denied to the one precisely because it has no next higher to which to relate, nor, indeed, can it be said to relate at all.[52] The one, then, eludes hypostatization. It must be thought otherwise; or more precisely, it does not lend itself to thinking at all. And yet, per-

---

anticipate the difference with the vocabulary of the *aiōnion* which names the way the soul is eternity-like.
47 Schürmann, *Broken Hegemonies*, 155.
48 *En.* III.7 [45], 6, 7–8.
49 Schürmann, *Broken Hegemonies*, 140.
50 See Hans Jonas, "The Soul in Gnosticism and Plotinus," in *Philosophical Essays: From Ancient Creed to Technoligical Man* (Chicago: The University of Chicago Press, 1974), 325–26.
51 See ibid., 333.
52 Plotinus writes: "But we must say that it is wholly unrelated to anything; for he is what he is before them for we take away the 'is', and so any way of relation to beings" (*En.* VI.8 [39], 12–15).

haps the very attempt to theorize eternity opens us to experience the originary temporality of the one as the singular event of union, an event that might be said to appear in every relation — in every "phenomenal constellating."[53]

To discern the one as the singular event of union, Schürmann enters into dialogue with the most difficult and important question in Plotinus: "how, from the one, if it is such as we say it is, anything else, be it a multitude, a dyad, or a number, came into existence, and how it did not remain there by itself...?"[54] If the metaphysics of explanatory causes seeks in the transcendent Intelligence an ultimate referent that answers to the question *why*, the question concerning how the one did not remain there by itself opens the site of a "second transcendence" that is no longer metaphysical, but rather, properly phenomenological.[55] Schürmann puts it this way:

> Plotinus takes a step backwards from this *metaphysical* difference between substantiality and things, a step which leads to the one.... What appears with this step can be called the *phenomenological* difference. The phenomenological difference secures no supreme ground, nothing which transcends a deficient reality toward a complete reality. It is only the transcendental condition of appearing.[56]

The phenomenological difference articulates the temporality exhibited in the event of appearing itself. The difference between eternity and everlastingness remains ultimately a metaphysical difference insofar as it grounds psychic time. Even so,

---

53 Schürmann, *Broken Hegemonies*, 148.
54 *En.* v.1 [10], 6, 5–8.
55 Schürmann speaks of this "second transcendence" as a "backward step which is incomparable to the first," the step from Soul to Intelligence. The second transcendence surpasses the Intelligence in a manner that cannot be thought as continuous with the first transcendence. The relation between the one and the Intelligence is strictly heterogeneous with that between the Intelligence and the Soul. See Schürmann, *Broken Hegemonies*, 140–41, 149.
56 Ibid., 146.

the attempt to articulate this ground brings the event of appearing itself to language in a twofold way. At the beginning, the event of appearing is articulated according to the nuptial union between the soul and eternity, a union that comes to expression in the middle voice with the participle *theōmenos*. At the end, the event of appearing is heard in the way eternity comes to presence as everlastingness which expresses how eternity is concealed in its very appearing. This way of self-manifesting too comes to expression in the middle voice, there with the participle *emphainomenēs*. When, however, the ultimate metaphysical reference of the Intelligence is denied, as it must be when the paradigm of the eternal is sought, the return that is theorizing and the procession that is manifestation are exposed to a phenomenological difference that reveals the originary temporality of the one as an event of union.

This event of union has been described as nuptial and in Plotinus it comes to language wherever he seeks to articulate the experience of union with the one. This, however, marks a second transcendence beyond Intelligence where "theorizing" or even "seeing" no longer suffices to articulate the union itself. Rather, the union is expressed with another participle in the middle voice, this time, however, it is articulated in the perfect tense, indicating completed aspect — thus suggesting complete repose and rest: *hēnōmenon*, united. This word voices the experience of union. Plotinus attempts to bring this experience to language in the treatise Porphyry places at the end of the *Enneads*:

> Since, then, there were not two, but the seer himself was one with the seen — for it was not really seen, but united [*hēnōmenon*] — if he should remember who he was when he was joined [*emignuto*] there, he will have an image of that in himself.[57]

---

[57] *En.* VI.9 [9], 11, 6–8. The term translated as "joined" connotes the mixing of liquids and thus a thorough intermingling in which the self dissolves as it experiences the event of union with the one.

According to Schürmann, this way of being *hēnōmenon*, which he himself risks reifying by appealing repeatedly to the substantive *hēnōsis*,[58] arises when the self "simplifies [*haplēsis*]," and "gives itself over [*epidosis*]" and presses toward "contact [*haphē*]" and comes to a "rest [*stasis*]."[59] Then, Schürmann suggests, "we are in communion with the one and originary 'time' (in quotes to suggest the model of the model of time, the life of the Soul)."[60] Here Schürmann insists that a certain natality is at stake, yet it is other than the natality that is the trait associated with maximization. To distinguish this other natality from maximizing natality, Schürmann speaks of "pure natality": "The one as singular event of union is natality — not maximized, but retained in its purity...."[61] Yet the very meaning of "event" in Schürmann, undermines the possibility of articulating the singular even of union as "pure natality." Rather, as an event, this other natality must be thought together with mortality, for the event of union is precisely *singular* and thus marked by a withdrawal that never comes to pure presence.

This is the underlying significance of Schürmann's own appeal in *Broken Hegemonies* to the Heideggerian understanding of *Ereignis* as he attempts to articulate the meaning of event itself. For Schürmann, *Ereignis* "may be translated as 'event,' so long as we understand by this both appropriation and expropriation." He goes on to say:

> The "proper" (*eigen*) points to the way singulars belong to one another in a world, a mutual belonging which is always made fragile from within by the *ex-* of expropriation (by the

---

58 This is a legitimate Plotinian term, one that appears perhaps more often than the perfect participle, *hēnōmenon*. The perfect participle appears also at: *En.* VI.5 [23], 5, 9 where Plotinus uses the image of the center of the circle to articulate the oneness of all things; and at *En.* VI.6 [34], 9, 29 where being is described as "unified number" [*arithmos hēnōmenos*] in order to insist upon the priority of the one even to being and number.
59 *En.* VI.9 [9], 11, 23ff.
60 Schürmann, *Broken Hegemonies*, 156.
61 Ibid.

Ent- of *Entzug*, etc.). The proper thus designates the movement by which things render themselves mutually and provisionally proximate — which does not mean unfailingly close by, or fully present.[62]

As *Ereignis*, the singular event of union cannot be said to signify pure natality. Rather, *Ereignis* articulates the nuptial insofar as it expresses the swell of appropriation together with the undertow of expropriation, the discordant union between a natality that is mortal, and a mortality that is natal.

In his attempt to articulate the nature of eternity, Plotinus engages in a kind of apophantic saying that brings the nuptial event of union to language. The fragility proper to nuptial union finds expression in the middle voice: *theōmenos, emphainomenēs, hēnōmenon*. With *theōmenos*, we hear the discordant union of ascending return which, when translated into the language of *Broken Hegemonies*, gives voice to the natality of mortality. This theorizing is mortal insofar as it involves a detachment from worldly things and a turn inward and upward toward the one that singularizes; yet it is also natal insofar as this return accomplishes a union with that which lies within and above. With *emphainomenēs*, we hear the discordant union of descending procession which gives voice to the mortality of natality. This appearing is natal insofar as it expresses the entering into constellation of phenomena; yet it is also mortal insofar as it marks the showing forth of each constellation as conditioned by an irreducible withdrawal. With *hēnōmenon*, we hear not pure natality, but the nuptial: the singular event of union in which the gathering of phenomena into relation is conditioned at once by natal mortality and mortal natality.

---

62 Ibid., 153. *Ereignis* must be thought in relation to *eignen*, which means to own and thus gives the sense of what is proper. The English *appropriation/expropriation*, must be heard in this context. For a discussion of *Ereignis* in relation to this rich set of meanings, see Heidegger, *Unterwegs zur Sprache*, 246. For a discussion of the English translations of these terms, see Martin Heidegger, *Basic Writings from Being and Time (1927) to The Task of Thinking (1964)*, vol. 2nd (New York: Harper & Row, 1993), 396.

Plotinus's thinking thus gives voice not to the purity of natality, but to a natality that shows itself as discordantly united with mortality. Even if what Schürmann's text says is "pure natality" purged of the trait of mortality,[63] in the now of our hermeneutical encounter with Schürmann and, through him, with Char and Plotinus, the natal and the mortal do communicate, not, indeed, to institute yet another hegemonic principle of ultimate authority, but to open a world in which a new possibility for acting appears in the wake of the nuptial union that comes to expression each time phenomena enter into relation. This new possibility for acting, however, is heard most acutely in Schürmann's reading of *Ennead* VI.8, *On the Freedom and Will of the One,* where he ultimately attends to "the labor of mortality" in the one itself and thus brings to language the mortality that shows itself as discordantly united with natality.[64]

The Feverish Advance

If the path to time begins, for Plotinus, with the theorizing that offers a direct experience of eternity in order to follow the pro-

---

63 Schürmann, *Broken Hegemonies,* 156. To be gentle and generous, Schürmann's appeal to "pure natality" is designed to purge natality of its maximizing strategies, and perhaps not to purge it of mortality itself. However, the course of the critique offered here suggests that Schürmann does not risk thinking the nuptial in *Broken Hegemonies,* but leaves that difficult project to those of us who, entering into hermeneutical relation with his texts, allow themselves to be interpreted by them.

64 As will be heard at the end of chapter four, the chiasmus between natal mortality and mortal natality is said to express a philosophy to come. The mortality of natality injects a dimension of openness and instability into the natal gathering of community while the natality of mortality articulates the communication endemic to mortal dispersion. By situating the poetics of politics at the site of nuptial union, this chapter seeks to draw out the political implications of the philosophy to come articulated in *The Voice of Singularity* by bringing it into relation with the sense of poetics found in *The Duplicity of Beginning.* It settles itself thus here in the middle of the book as a singular event of union, the middle panel of a triptych that unites *The Duplicity of Beginning* together with *The Voice of Singularity,* the morning light together with the dusk of night.

cession into time, the path to the freedom and the will of the one is yet more audacious. Unlike in the treatise on time, here Plotinus begins with us and with what is "in our power" even as he insists: "we must dare [*tolmēteon*] to enquire of the first things and of that which is up beyond all things, and in this sort of way enquire, even if we agree that all things are possible for him, how it is in his power."[65] This enquiry marks a feverish advance beyond the metaphysics of archic domination by daring to articulate *the free will of the one in the one*.[66] Here Plotinus relinquishes the apophatic discourse on the one in order to risk speaking cataphatically. He thus allows himself to "follow along with the words," recognizing that they are, strictly speaking, not permitted to be deployed in the manner he is risking and thus must always be heard along with a decisive "as if" (*hoion*).[67]

---

65 *En.* VI.8 [39], 1, 9–11.
66 This formulation itself shows what is at stake. Schürmann insists that the "and" in the title of the tractate, *On the Freedom and Will of the One*, must be read as "that is to say" so that the title designates already the *free will* of the one. See Schürmann, *Broken Hegemonies*, 183. The genitive, "of" in the sentence above, however, is doubled in a way that undermines the attempt to understand the one's willing as the positing of an ultimate law. Schürmann puts it this way: "For the one to be one, the free willing 'of' the one (subjective genitive) must keep its distance 'from' (objective genitive) the one which it wills and posits. If that distance were obliterated in a uniformly successful theticism, therefore in some First taking pleasure in itself fully, that would be the undoing of love. The double genitive function spoils thetic simplicity." See ibid., 182. In order, however, to articulate how this double function of the genitive does not introduce a duplicity into the one itself, Schürmann finds recourse in the dative: "Rather than positing the other of the one we have to try to think the other in the one. If we do not, we will come to the conclusion…that there is a 'dualism of principles' in the one." See ibid., 648.
67 *En.* VI.8 [39], 13, 47–50. Armstrong recognizes this treatise as the one in which Plotinus articulates the one "in more strongly positive terms than anywhere else in the Enneads." See Plotinus, Armstrong, and Porphyry, *Plotinus*, vol. VII, 223. Leroux emphasizes that "Plotinus allows himself to go so far as to ask about the freedom of the One itself" and goes on to suggest that this seems like a "damning question." See Georges Leroux, "Human Freedom in the Thought of Plotinus," in *The Cambridge Companion to Plotinus*, ed. Lloyd P. Gerson (New York: Cambridge University Press, 1996), 294.

Here an echo of Aristotle is heard; for, as emphasized in chapter 2, Aristotle used the pronoun *ti* and the adverb *pōs* to gesture to the indefiniteness at play in the being of the one.[68] This is a language attentive to dispersion; it signals a heuristic of dysfunction — precisely there, where the limits of language are felt, something other than the conceptual shows itself. This happens only, however, as Plotinus risks a certain audacity: to articulate free willing in the one. Daring to speak cataphatically, Plotinus's language becomes apophantic, capable of showing that "originary audacity fractures archic simplicity."[69] By following along with the words that seek to articulate free willing in the one, Plotinus brings the trait of mortality to language, indeed, suffers the "labor of mortality," and in so doing, shows the event of its discordant union with natality: the nuptial.

Thus, Plotinus gives voice not only, as Schürmann insists, to the destitution of the ancient hen-fantasm, but also to the diremption of the history of etiological metaphysics itself, despite its continuation over the course of what is soon to be two millennia. Schürmann's reading of Plotinus shows this, even if it continues to speak of only of destitution.[70] If, however, in Schürmann's hermeneutic engagement with Plotinus, the expiration of the economy of thetic maximization is heard, it is because Plotinus himself has the audacity to bring the free will of the one to language, an audacity that shows the event of discordant

---

68 See the discussion of *Metaphysics* VIII in chapter 2, above. *Meta.*, VIII.6, 1045b17–21.

69 See Schürmann, *Broken Hegemonies*, 174.

70 It is tempting to deploy a Schürmannian trope against Schürmann himself and say about him what he has said about Aquinas, Kant, and others: that he succeeds in instituting the topological analytic of ultimates in *Broken Hegemonies* by denying the manner in which Plotinian thinking already dirempts the metaphysics of maximizing ultimates. This diremption, of course, comes too soon for Schürmann — indeed, just as Aristotle seems to come too soon for Hegel — and so, it is posited as a mere destitution that gives rise to the Latin hegemony of nature. Yet, even if Schürmann's phenomenology of epochal history shows how the Latin fantasm was instituted after this end of the Greek beginning, Plotinus announces a diremption: he gives voice to an expiration of metaphysical theticism itself and not just the destitution of the hen-fantasm.

union itself. To trace the nuptial in Plotinus then, it will be necessary to attend first to the way he articulates the free will of the one in the one in order then to hear how Schürmann's reading of this apophantic saying brings the nuptial itself to language as *alētheia* — "the conflictual, agonal truth of the one."[71]

Throughout much of the treatise on the freedom and will of the one, Plotinus remains bound to the metaphysics of etiological ultimates. This is, perhaps, the result of the path this text undertakes, moving from what "being in our power" (*eph' hēmin*) and willing means for us in order to discern something of the power of the one and its willing. Even as he presses forward to the good and the one in chapter seven and begins to deploy the "as if" (*hoion*) that allows his language to point beyond the conceptual, he remains loyal to a set of metaphors that fail to carry us beyond the foundational economy of metaphysical ultimates. Thus, in chapter fifteen we hear that the one is "like the principle [*archē*] and foundation [*basis*] of a great tree living according to *logos*, for it remains itself by itself, giving to the tree being according to *logos*, which it receives."[72] The *archē* here is identified with a foundation that serves its traditional metaphysical function as the ultimate principle of order, itself unconditioned and covertly legitimatized by the ascription of goodness to the order it produces. Even if the organic metaphor of the unfolding root can be heard to gesture to an immanent power capable of subverting the logic of domination endemic to the metaphysics of fabrication, this power is eclipsed immediately by the architectural connotations of the *basis* with which the principle is identified. As architectural, the principle functions as the ultimate foundation of the world order and thus fails to articulate the discontinuity endemic to the freedom of the one.[73]

---

71 Schürmann, *Broken Hegemonies*, 187.
72 *En.* VI.8 [39], 15, 34–37.
73 Schürmann points to the limits of the metaphors of "emanation" in Plotinus: "According to this metaphor, the principle would remain in itself, rich and overabundant like a headwater, and yet it would pour out by an intrinsic necessity. There is no headwater without water flowing from it. To speak of emanation is thus to connect the principle to the world. Now if

In chapter eighteen, however, Plotinus advances a metaphor that comes closer to affirming the freedom and thus the otherness of the one. Here, the one is said to be "like light widely dispersed from some one, transparent in itself." Although it disperses light, the one is in itself unseen. Its power is everywhere but itself, strictly speaking, nowhere — for *there* all place has been excluded: the one offers thinking no *topos* for its *logos* to grasp.[74] Thus, Plotinus is compelled to speak poetically, to gesture to the one in metaphorical language capable of carrying thinking beyond the conceptual to the singular which, in showing itself, remains unseen. This is the importance of the transparency "in itself" of the one. Plotinus puts it poignantly elsewhere when he imagines the one as a small luminous mass at the center of a transparent sphere and then, abstracting the mass and leaving only "the light as power," he suggests: "but the light would be at once everywhere one and the same, having for itself no beginning [*archexamenon*] and having no beginning anywhere."[75] Here the metaphor of light as power without *archē* gestures to the otherness of the one even as it affirms a certain communication with all that otherwise exists. Returning, then, to the passage from VI.8 [39], 18, we find this otherness which shows itself coming to language in terms of truth, *alēthes*: "what

---

Plotinus is the first to sketch a thought of freedom, it is precisely to preserve the one from all these connections and the ties binding it to what is other than itself." See Schürmann, *Broken Hegemonies*, 141. Armstrong has suggested that the metaphors of emanation in Plotinus "conceal a confusion of thought under a cloud of metaphors." See A.H. Armstrong, "'Emanation' in Plotinus," *Mind* 46 (1937): 61–66, at 61. Rather than thematizing such metaphors hubristically as covering "a confusion of thought," it might be best to think of these metaphors more literally as attempts to carry us beyond the order of thetic maximizations — metaphors that breakdown in heuristically important ways.

74 *En.* VI.8 [39], 11, 13ff. There Plotinus insists that the one cannot be understood topologically by positing first a *topos* or even a *chora* in which to situate the one, for "that place, like everything else, is afterwards, and last of all afterwards."

75 *En.* VI.4 [22], 7, 23–47. The reflexive "for itself" is here again designed to bring the middle voice of the Greek participle to language in English.

is dispersed is image, but that from which it comes is truth."[76] In speaking here of the one as truth, *alēthes,* Plotinus gestures to the sense of the one as event of self-concealing presencing.[77] According to Schürmann, the light metaphor has the advantage of being able to suggest the possibility of communication without a diminution of the one. He continues: "The metaphor is good for emphasizing the otherness of the second transcendence, so long as it conceives of our world as a non-isotropic realm."[78] With the metaphor of light as pure power omnipresent and yet beyond the order of metaphysical beginnings, Plotinus attempts to give voice to the one as that which is at work everywhere and yet not as a principle of ultimate domination — its activity, as will be heard, is *poetic,* not in the sense of production, but as an *event of discordant union.* The articulation of the one as *alēthes* suggests already the dynamics of the event that is the one.

Even so, however, Plotinus cannot extricate himself from the metaphysics of causes so easily. The moment he touches upon the otherness of the one, he moves to reassert its continuity with the hypostatic Intelligence, which is a "dispersed image" though not "an alien form [*alloeides*]."[79] The attempt to insist upon the

---

76 *En.* VI.8 [39], 18, 33–36. Truth here must already be heard to articulate the dynamic event of union. Only thus heard can the metaphor of emanation be thought together with Plotinus's insistence on omnipresence so that the one can be said to emanate from a transparent center *and yet also* be present in every constellation of appearing. Armstrong's insistence that the metaphor of emanation be relinquished as inadequate in the face of the adoption of a robust theory of omnipresence fails to think the one as dynamic event of union. Even so, however, Armstrong seems to recognize that something important is at stake when Plotinus appeals to *dunamis* to articulate the omnipresence of the one. See Armstrong, "'Emanation' in Plotinus," 62.

77 This is, of course, a Heideggerian formulation rooted in his late understanding of the meaning of *alētheia* as "the opening of presence concealing itself, the opening of a self-concealing sheltering." See Martin Heidegger, *On Time and Being* (New York: Harper and Row, 1972), 71. Although Heidegger does not seem to have Plotinus in mind in this text, one of his more poignant formulations resonates strongly with Plotinian thinking: "We must think aletheia, unconcealment, as the opening which first grants Being and thinking and their presencing to and for each other." See ibid., 68.

78 Schürmann, *Broken Hegemonies,* 141.

79 *En.* VI.8 [39], 18, 36–37.

ultimate eidetic continuity of things, however, is not permitted to give rise to another in a long line of systems founded upon the metaphysics of form. Even so, this does not prevent Plotinus from articulating the one in terms of an etiological economy of which it itself is no part:

> [B]ut that there [*ekeino*] is the cause of the cause. It is then in a greater degree something like [*hoion*] the most causative [*aitiōtaton*] and truer [*alēthesteron*] cause, holding together all things about to be from it, it will be the intellective causes and generative of what is, not as it happened to be, but as he himself willed.[80]

Here Plotinus gives expression to the henological maximization this thinking announces as expired. The statement is shot through with a tension conceptual language cannot tolerate. This tension is heard in the articulation of the *hoion*, "something like," which voices the discontinuity between the economy of causes and the will of the one. It is felt in the excess of language that posits the one first as the superlative cause only then to go further by announcing a comparative, a truer cause. This excess of language — a cause truer than the most causative — marks the step beyond the economy of causes itself. Plotinus himself insists in chapter nineteen that this step beyond the metaphysics of ontological causes is the truth of the "dark saying by the ancients" which spoke of that which is "beyond being [*epekeina ousias*]."[81] In fleshing out the truth of this dark saying, Plotinus gives voice at once to the enigmatic will of the one and to a *poiēsis* other than that of ontological production.

The key formula that marks the rupture between ontological etiology and the freedom of the one is heard here, immediately after Plotinus invokes the dark saying of the *Republic* that points beyond *ousia* and thus beyond all ousiology. For Plotinus, this saying means:

---

80 *En.* VI.8 [39], 18, 38–42.
81 *En.* VI.8 [39], 19, 13–15.

[N]ot only that he generates *ousia*, but that he is not a slave to *ousia* or to himself, nor is the beginning in him the *ousia* of him, but he, being the beginning of *ousia*, did not make [*epoiēse*] *ousia* in himself, but making [*poiēsas*] it, he let it be outside himself [*exō eiasen*], because he has no need of being, he who made [*epoiēsen*] it.[82]

This passage articulates a peculiar sort of poetics. It is the poetics of the simple freedom of the one in the one. Plotinus moves decisively beyond ousiology with the formulation that the one is not a slave to *ousia*, emphasizing the utter singularity of the one and its independence from the economy of domination by refusing to bring the one even under the authority of itself. The verb *poieō* is then articulated three times in the aorist tense, enunciating the simplicity of the making endemic to this freedom. Here a peculiar sort of temporality is heard, for the aorist marks the simple past with simple aspect. Eloquently, it articulates a singular occurrence once. The appearance of the aorist participle between the two finite iterations of *poieō* gestures to an antecedent making that expresses something like the temporality of the one — it expresses a simple making prior to all making, a making that remains outside the economy of production.[83] The free willing of the one is thus a simple poetic making that lets-be, a simple gathering that, in gathering, withdraws.

Plotinus seeks to clarify the meaning of this other making by speaking in temporal terms, drawing on verb tenses to express the difference between one making and another. In chapter twenty, he writes:

Now if there were a time when he began to be, the "to have made" [*to pepoiēkenai*] would be said in its most proper

---

[82] *En.* VI.8 [39], 19, 15–19.
[83] Smyth insists that "the action set forth by the aorist participle is generally antecedent to that of the leading verb...." See Smyth, *Greek Grammar,* 420, §1872c. Plotinus emphasizes that this making remains outside the metaphysics of being in the very next sentence: "He does not even make [*poiēi*] being according to his being" (*En.* VI.8 [39], 19, 20).

> sense. But now, if he indeed was [*ēn*] before eternity [*prin aiōna*] existed, this "to have made" itself must be thought to be a concurrence of the "to have made" and the self, for the to be is one with the making and a sort of everlasting generation [*hoion gennēsi aidiō*].[84]

This passage gives voice to a temporal difference between the one and Intelligence that echoes the temporal difference that came to language between the Intelligence and the Soul. With the so-called philosophical imperfect (*ēn*), which here points to that which is prior even to the temporality determined as eternal, Plotinus attempts to think the poetics of the one as a kind of concurrence with itself, a making that is audaciously articulated as "a sort of everlasting generation." With the shift from *prin aiōna* to *hoion gennēsi aidiō*, from a "before eternity" to "a sort of everlasting generation," Plotinus articulates the temporal difference endemic to the freedom of the one.

> Thus, ultimately, Plotinus thinks the freedom of the one as a dynamic event:
> For the ability to make there is not to be thought as the power to make the opposites, but as a power unshaken and settled [*astemphei kai ametakinētōi*], which is most of all power when it does not go out of the one; for to be capable of the opposites is an incapacity to remain with the best. But it is necessary that his making, of which we speak, itself be once for all [*hapax*].[85]

Here Plotinus speaks the language of Aristotle to articulate the *dunamis* of the one. Where Aristotle says *bebaiōs kai ametakinētōs* to articulate the manner in which virtue settles into the soul and becomes a stable, active condition that can't be moved all the way to its opposite, Plotinus says *astemphei kai*

---

84 *En.* VI.8 [39], 20, 23–27.
85 *En.* VI.8 [39], 21, 3–8.

ametakinētōi to articulate the activity of the one itself.[86] It is as if its way of being, or *hexis,* is a dynamic event beyond the economy of opposites that characterizes the etiological metaphysics of archic domination. Thus, it is not enough to understand the one negatively as unity beyond *ousia,* but in daring to speak cataphatically about the free will of the one in the one, Plotinus gives voice to the one as the singular event of union — that is, he gives voice to the nuptial.

Schürmann's reading recognizes this, even if he does not here speak in terms of the nuptial itself. Rather, the nuptial in *Broken Hegemonies* remains shrouded by too dichotomous an economy of relation between natality and mortality. Even so, the nuptial comes to language as Schürmann enters into hermeneutical relation with Plotinus in an attempt to think the one as singular event of union. It may be heard, then, in those passages in which Schürmann articulates the one as both uniting and simplifying together. Strikingly, these passages suggest the broader, political implications of the Plotinian attempt to speak the free will of the one in the one; for by bringing the one to language as singularizing and uniting *at once,* Plotinus allows the *dynamics* of appearing to show itself. This sort of apophantic saying awakens us to the peculiar poetics that conditions all gathering — the simple making that lets-be announced in the very attempt to bring the free willing of the one to language. This awakening opens the path to another acting, one rooted in and attuned to the making endemic to nuptial union. To discern something of this other acting, it will be necessary to attend to those passages in Schürmann's reading of Plotinus that speak of the singular

---

86 Aristotle, *Aristotelis Ethica Nicomachea* (Oxford: Oxford University Press, 1894), 11.4, 1105a33. Sachs has a very good account of the importance of the adverbs *bebaiōs,* "stably" or "having taken a stand," and *ametakinētōs,* which Sachs translates as: "being in a condition from which one can't be moved all the way over into a different condition." See Joe Sachs, *Aristotle: Nicomachean Ethics* (Newburyport: Focus Publishing, 2002), xiii and 26n30. Given the appearance of the Aristotelian vocabulary in Plotinus, it is clear that he is trying to articulate something like the active condition (*hexis*) of the one itself.

event of union; for there the nuptial is heard as the site of the poetics of politics.

For Those Who Stumble in the Morning Heaviness

Let us return, here at the end of this middle panel, as the evening twilight makes its inevitable approach, to the beginning. Let us return, specifically, to the symbol of the "morning heaviness" that announces the end of Char's poem and the world opened by it. This symbol, Schürmann says, translates "Char's dream of unity. The morning is the hour of rising, of innocent beginning, of the gull. Heaviness is of the impenetrable sea, of the house, of the shark. As if a lightening flash, the poem makes me a unifier."[87] Here an important reversal that anticipates the chiasmus between natal mortality and mortal natality is heard. Earlier the gull was said to be "constant leaving" and "vertical flight," traits associated with mortality. Here, however, the gull symbolizes a sort of beginning. Earlier the shark was said to "settle in the depth, gravity is its shelter." These images evoke the natal. Here, however, the shark symbolizes an impenetrability associated with the trait of mortality. Thus, the gull must be heard to symbolize the natality of mortality, the shark, the mortality of natality. The nuptial of the gull and shark, then, expresses a chiastic union: the natality of mortality joins discordantly with the mortality of natality.

If the symbol of morning heaviness brings the nuptial of the gull and shark to language in Char, perhaps the symbol of the one as the singular event of union may be heard to bring the nuptial of natality and mortality to language in Schürmann. To stumble in the morning heaviness, then, will be to act in the wake of the nuptial without denying the discord that conditions nuptial gathering itself. Such acting will be of necessity symbolic, its politics, poetic.

The symbolic praxis of poetic politics is rooted not in archic domination, but in an ability to remain attuned and responsive

---

87 Schürmann, "Situating René Char," 518.

to the nuptial. Schürmann suggests how the nuptial, which he continues to think in terms of a certain natality, both announces itself in Plotinus and always already conditions human being in the world of appearing. He begins with this: "Simplification and union in Plotinus thus constitutes the essential traits both of man and the one. This is why the latter is best described by processes: not just 'uniting' (*henoein*) but also 'letting-be' (*eaein*)."[88] Schürmann associates this letting-be with the Plotinian insistence upon gentleness. Plotinus himself says that "the Good is gentle and mild" and that the things of this world should not be reviled, but "one should rather calmly and gently accept the nature of all things, and hurry on oneself to the first."[89] This gentleness, however, may itself be heard as a kind of response to what Schürmann has called the originary audacity of the one that "fractures archic simplicity," an audacity that the attempt to articulate the free will of the one brings to a language that shatters etiological metaphysics.[90] This audacity, to be sure, is not the audacity Plotinus himself condemns as the rash speaking of maladjusted people,[91] nor, however, is it strictly speaking, the audacity Plotinus associates first with the Intelligence as it "somehow dared to stand away from the one" and then, descending further, with the souls which have the audacity that is "coming to birth and the first otherness and the wishing to belong to themselves."[92] For Schürmann, "audacity must be thought

---

88 Schürmann, *Broken Hegemonies*, 157.
89 For the first quotation, see *En.* v.5 [32], 12, 33–35; for the second, see II.9 [33], 13, 6–7.
90 See Schürmann, *Broken Hegemonies*, 174. In an interesting and thorough study of tolma in Plotinus, Torchia links the willing of the one with its causal activity and thus fails to recognize the degree to which the audacity of the one explodes the causal economy. See N. Joseph Torchia, *Plotinus, Tolma, and the Descent of Being: An Exposition and Analysis* (New York: P. Lang, 1993), 100.
91 See *En.* VI.8 [39], 7, 11.
92 For the daring of Intellegence, see *En.* VI.9 [9], 5, 29–30. This *tolma* is associated with what Plotinus describes as unfolding of time with the restless nature of the Intelligence: "But since there was a restless, active nature which wanted to control itself and be on its own, and chose to seek for more that its present state, this moved and with it time moved" (*En.* III.7 [45], 11,

otherwise than as negation. It emphasizes the principle of overabundance throughout the entire hypostatic architecture."[93] Schürmann names this other audacity, "originary audacity" as he attempts to articulate the willing in the one that gives voice not merely to the conflict between two laws in differend, but to the discordant union that describes the singularizing dynamic of appearing itself.

The dynamics at play here are decidedly not those at work in the metaphysics of etiological oppositions. Indeed, Schürmann is careful to insist that Plotinus's articulation of the power of willing in the one does not operate within the logic of Aristotle's opposition between *energeia* and *dunamis* but the two converge in the willing of the one.[94] Thus, the power of the one is not in the service of an ultimate authority. Schürmann calls this power "anarchic," suggesting that

> a dissension belabors the one from within. It lacks a simple essence. The *archê* is not all its own. It is anarchic by virtue of an act of otherness which troubles it. Phenomenological anarchism always results from an originary act of *différend* between conditions.[95]

14–17. Jonas suggests this association in a note, describing tolma signifying "the particularization of the Soul from the One." Jonas, "Plotin über Ewigkeit und Zeit," 314. For a more detailed discussion of this connection, albeit one that remains too wedded a reading of Plotinus through the dichotomy of the optimistic and the pessimistic, see Torchia, *Plotinus, Tolma, and the Descent of Being: An Exposition and Analysis*, 103–4. For a critique of the manner in which Torchia reads tolma into almost all the so-called pessimistic texts of Plotinus, see Andrew Smith, "Review: Tolma in Plotinus," *The Classical Review* 46, no. 1 (1996): 76–78. For the audacity associated with souls, see: *En.* v.1 [10], 1, 4–6.

93 Schürmann, *Broken Hegemonies*, 184.

94 For a good discussion of the difference between the Aristotelian and Plotinian understanding of the dynamis/energeia relation, particularly as it relates to the one beyond being (*au-delà de l'être*), see Jean-Marc Narbonne, *La Métaphysique de Plotin* (Paris: Librairie Philosophique J. Vrin, 1994), 26–38.

95 Schürmann, *Broken Hegemonies*, 163–64. See too, 648n54 and 166.

Yet this phenomenological anarchism remains apophatic insofar as it expresses the "closure of metaphysics," to use Derrida's language.[96] Anarchy articulates this apophatically by exposing a dissension that belabors the one from within, descending into the hypostatic order by the original but already refracted audacity of the Intelligence that dares to stand out from the one. As apophatic, this anarchism expresses only the dimension of the nuptial that withdraws and not the duplicity of the nuptial itself as singular event of discordant union. In so doing, however, anarchy gestures to the trace of an originary discordant union that is always already at play in every gathering.[97]

Thus, it is precisely because Schürmann refuses to describe the legislative double bind endemic to all archic theticism in exclusively negative terms and instead risks speaking audaciously about the singular event of union that "occurs whenever there is appearing," that what is said in *Broken Hegemonies*, particularly

---

96 Jacques Derrida, *Margins of Philosophy*, trans. Alan Bass (Chicago: University of Chicago Press, 1982), 172.

97 Rist has emphasized that one of Plotinus's favorite metaphors to gesture to the complete transcendence of the one is that of the trace. See John M. Rist, *Plotinus: The Road to Reality* (Cambridge: Cambridge University Press, 1967), 27–28. Derrida associates the audacity of the *Enneads* themselves with this trace as it gives voice to a certain presence or, if we must use the language of metaphysics against itself, to a formless form. Plotinus says: "The trace of the shapeless is shape [*to gar ikhnos tou amorphou morphē*]" (*En.* VI.7 [38], 33, 30). Drawing on this, Derrida says: "In a sense — or non-sense — that metaphysics would have excluded from its field, while nevertheless remaining in secret and incessant relation with this sense, form in itself already would be the trace (*ikhnos*) of a certain nonpresence, the vestige of the un-formed, which announces-recalls its other, as did Plotinus, perhaps, for all of metaphysics. The trace would not be the mixture, the transition between form and the amorphous, presence and absence, etc., but that which, by eluding this opposition, makes it possible in the irreducibility of its excess." See Derrida, *Margins of Philosophy*, 172. *Broken Hegemonies* remains therapeutic in the sense — or non-sense — that it assiduously exposes the secret and incessant relation to nonpresence the metaphysics of presence covers over in positing its own authority. Yet if we audaciously attempt to follow this trace, to respond to it with an apophantic saying capable of bringing it to a certain expression, something more than the therapeutic becomes possible: the poetics of politics.

as Schürmann enters into hermeneutical relation with Plotinus, can give voice to the nuptial as the originary discordant union of natality and mortality. In a passage that resonates with the lightening flash in which the "poem makes me a unifier," Schürmann emphasizes that the free will of the one happens at once, *hapax*, as an event. "Literally a 'flash', for union is always made suddenly (*exaiphnes*). It is an instant out of time, which is not simple — the strategy of centering on the one (natality) is allied with the *contre-temps* which singularization (mortality) is."[98] This alliance is the nuptial itself.

In *Broken Hegemonies,* the nuptial comes to language most poignantly as Schürmann appeals to the appearance of the word *alētheia* in a passage from chapter fourteen of *On the Freedom and Will of the One*. Although he suggests, wrongly, that Plotinus does not allow us to dwell on the word because he "uses the word *alêtheia* just once,"[99] Schürmann insists that we attend carefully to what *alētheia* says in that text. Listen first to the passage from Plotinus:

> [E]ach of the things which according to truth [*kata alētheian*] are and has come into existence from that nature [the one], even if it is a certain sort of perceptible thing, is the sort of thing it is from that [nature]. But with respect to "a thing of this sort" I mean: to have together with their *ousia* also the cause of their existence.[100]

Schürmann interprets the text this way:

> In other words, it matters little if one speaks about intelligible or sensible things (and it matters little what the etiological schema is), all plural beings possess their proper singular be-

---

98 Schürmann, *Broken Hegemonies,* 184.
99 Ibid., 187. We have already heard the truth appear twice: in *En.* VI.8 [39], 18, 36 and 39. In that tractate alone iterations of it appear at: 6, 39; 11, 35; 14, 33; 15, 25; and 21, 31 where it literally brings the text on the will to a conclusion by insisting that the one "alone is free in truth...".
100 *En.* VI.8, 14, 17–21.

ing and also the universal cause of being, a cause that is the one, origin of processions.[101]

For Schürmann, the importance of this passage lies in the way it invites us to think two sorts of union together in the one in terms of *alētheia*. He writes:

> [T]he dissension of concealment and unconcealment binds the two senses of union—as event of manifestation and as rapture. In manifestation, withdrawal means that an order of appearance gathers beings, but also is always already preparing to expel them and abandon them to their singularity; in rapture withdrawal demonstrates the soul as it frees itself from its form, passes beyond relation and difference, instantaneously beating a retreat. This idea "at once" (*exaiphnes*, suddenly), in which union is made, veils and splits asunder full presence just as it unveils it and lets it flash. Hence we have the conflictual, agonal truth of the one—as singularizing *contre-temps*, it devastates all forms and configurations to which it gives birth as the phenomenalizing event.[102]

As event of manifestation, *alētheia* expresses the dynamic of appearing itself; as event of rapture, *alētheia* articulates the peculiar manner in which souls are attuned to that dynamic as an event of discordant union in which they themselves always already participate.[103]

The nuptial event of union between natality and mortality that conditions appearing as such comes to language in Schürmann as conflictual, agonal truth. As an event of manifestation, truth appears wherever beings enter into constellation, a gathering always already ravaged by an ineluctable and elusive withdrawal. Schürmann's own formulation, however, amplifies

---

101 Schürmann, *Broken Hegemonies*, 187.
102 Ibid.
103 The site here described in terms of the conflictual, agonal truth was called in chapter two the "ravaged site of rapture." See too, Long, "The Duplicity of Beginning: Schürmann, Aristotle and the Origins of Metaphysics," 155–56.

the discordant dimension of the nuptial, thus muting it as simultaneously unifying. But truth as *alētheia* is not merely conflictual and agonal, expressing the undertow of mortality, it is also, unifying and communal, expressing the swell of natality. Something of its natality is heard, when Schürmann speaks of truth as an event of rapture in which souls become attuned to their own participation in the event of union that is phenomenal gathering. Only when the truth of mortality as natal is heard together with the truth of natality as mortal does the nuptial show itself as the site of poetic politics.

The path to the nuptial in which the poetics of politics is situated was opened by an apophantic saying as gentle as it was audacious. Along the way, however, something more has shown itself, for the very manner in which the nuptial offered itself in hermeneutical relation — to Char, to Plotinus, and, indeed, to Schürmann — suggests something about the nature of the poetics of politics itself. In each case, an attuned, responsive engagement with what was said in the texts set us on a path toward the nuptial that opened new constellations of meaning and new possibilities for community. Thus, the poetics of politics involves a certain symbolic praxis. This praxis, which may now be heard to refract Plotinus's originary poetic articulation of the one whose making is also a letting-be, announces the duplicitous gathering endemic to symbols. Symbols act and in so acting call for an attuned response, a sort of gentleness that allows phenomena to show themselves in their truth without imposing upon them a principle that sets them into order. Yet, if symbolic praxis invites a gentle attunement, it also requires a certain responsive audacity, one that refuses to remain silent in the wake of phenomenal gathering. Responsive audacity is rooted in the recognition that truth shows itself in, and may indeed be amplified by, the poetic attempt to articulate the very coming to presence of what shows itself.

The poetics of politics is the attuned response, as audacious as it is gentle, to the nuptial gathering of community. It is a praxis in the middle voice, for it eludes the strict dichotomy between agent and patient, the active and the passive, but situates itself between, at the site of the happening of truth, where natality is mortal and mortality natal. Its logic is chiastic, for its attunement is already response, its ability to respond already attunement. Its audacity is gentle, its gentleness audacious. Only such a chiastic logic can be apophantic, capable of somehow doing justice to the dynamic play of the showing itself, remaining attuned always to the singularities that elude all saying, a reminder of the mortality that conditions natality itself. The audacity of this poetic politics is gentle, for it attends carefully to that which withdraws in every gathering, allowing itself to be held open by the trace of mortality felt in wake of that withdrawal. Yet, its gentleness is audacious, for it does not permit the ineluctable and necessary elusiveness of gathering to deter its natal impulse to do justice to the truth that shows itself there. Apophantic saying is symbolic praxis in the middle voice, at once determined by nuptial gathering and determined to speak and act in dialogue with the truth that shows itself there. A poetic politics, situated thus at the site of discordant union, would then be capable of attending responsively to the happening of truth and responding attentively to the dynamic gathering that opens new possibilities of community for those who stumble in the morning heaviness.

4

Evening
The Voice of Singularity and a Philosophy to Come

Lead me, now, child,
to a place where, walking reverently, we
might speak and listen.
Let us not war with necessity.
  — Sophocles, *Oedipus Tyrannus,* Oedipus, ll. 188–91[1]

With the possible exception of Oedipus himself, no one stumbles more audaciously in the morning heaviness than Agamemnon at Aulis. Caught between two laws — as king, he must sacrifice his daughter to calm the winds at Aulis; as father, he must protect his child — Agamemnon could not inhabit the ravaged site of asymmetrical dialogue between natality and mortality; he could not abide the discord endemic to the site of nuptial union.[2] His was a negative, not an originary audacity.

---

1 Sophocles, *Sophoclis Fabulae* (Oxford: Clarendon Press, 1990).
2 An earlier version of this chapter was originally published as Christopher P. Long, "The Voice of Singularity and a Philosophy to Come: Schürmann, Kant and the Pathology of Being." *Philosophy Today* 53, no. Supplement (2009): 138–50.

At the very moment his ultimate sovereignty is secured, Agamemnon's voice trembles as one law is denied to allow the other to reign supreme. This is what Aeschylus has him say:

> For if this sacrifice, this virgin blood, stops the winds, it is right [*themis*] for them [his allies] to desire it with passion, most passionately [*orga periorgō sph' epithumein*]. May all be well.[3]

The poet's language captures the signature of Agamemnon's tragic denial. Aeschylus reduplicates the word *orgē*, which means at once violent emotion, anger, and passionate suffering, and thus articulates the force endemic to the institution of the univocal law. This orgy of language expresses both the *means* and the *manner* in which the law is established: As the law of the patriarchy is installed "with passion," the law of the father is "most passionately" denied.[4] This denial is amplified by the prefix *peri-*, which means "exceedingly," and so gives voice to a certain excess. This singular here, Iphigeniea, is sacrificed in the name of a divine *themis* appealed to by a King set on consolidating his authority absolute.[5] Yet the poet refuses to pass over this moment of rupture in silence. His language trembles and the tragic denial that institutes the law is exposed. In and through language, a rupture appears that undermines the ultimate authority of the patriarchal law.

The moment Agamemnon, voice trembling, denies his responsibility as father to assert his sovereignty as king is marked by what the Chorus calls "a most audacious change of mind [*to*

---

3 Aeschylus, J.D. Denniston, and Denys Lionel Page, *Agamemnon* (Oxford: Clarendon Press, 1960), ll. 214–17.
4 The Greek dative is capable of expressing both the means by which something is done and the manner in which it is done. See Herbert Weir Smyth, *Greek Grammar* (Cambridge: Harvard University Press, 1956), 346–48.
5 For a detailed interpretation of the manner in which Agamemnon's authority is established and the larger political implications of his tragic denial, see Christopher P. Long, "The Daughters of Metis: Patriarchal Dominion and the Politics of the Between," *The Graduate Faculty Philosophy Journal* 28, no. 2 (2007): 67–86.

pantotolmon phronein metagnō]."⁶ The audacity we encounter here is not the "originary audacity" of Plotinus, attuned to a power not in the service of an ultimate authority, but the negative audacity of the sovereign principle as it attempts — always ultimately in vain — to enforce the rule of its univocal law. This change of mind involves a deranged audacity that enables Agamemnon to somehow turn a deaf ear to the "pleading" and "terrified cries of Father" (228), to resist the way Iphigeneia fell upon his feet and grasped his robes (234–35), to deny his daughter's "last piteous look" (240). With each poignant detail, Aeschylus requires us to consider what is lost in the thetic act by which a univocal principle is won.

Yet even Aeschylus refuses to allow the Chorus to see or tell what happened next — the denial of the singular is shrouded in a silence that haunts the dominion of the univocal law. The legislative act entails the seeds of its own destruction. "Justice," however, "will tip the scales, to bring learning through suffering [*pathei mathos*]" (249–50). The thetic act by which Agamemnon secures his rule is tormented from the start by the suffering of the singular to which it will, in the end, owe justice — its demise is rooted already in its inception.

With Agamemnon and Iphigeneia at Aulis, we have arrived at darkest night; and yet there is even here a gesture to the dawn. Aeschylus has the chorus remind us of our finitude and of the morning light:

> With respect to the future, you will hear of it when
> it happens, until then, let it go [*chairetō*],
> it is like grieving in advance,
> it will arrive together with the light of dawn.⁷

With each act of tragic denial, there is an anticipated awakening; natality is mortal — Agamemnon kills Iphigeneia, Oedipus attempts to evade his fate. But mortality too is natal — Orestes

---

6 Aeschylus, Denniston, and Page, *Agamemnon*, l. 221.
7 Ibid., ll. 250–54.

will find sanctuary in Athens, the Furies will be honored as Eumenides, and Oedipus will find refuge in their sacred grove with his two daughters, somehow having learned through suffering to inhabit the nuptial site of discordant union.

To the grove of the Eumenides, then, we must follow the path of Schürmann's thinking in order to perhaps discern there the habits of nuptial response-ability that condition the possibility of a poetic politics. The echo of another trembling voice leads the way.

The Trace of a Denial

In a 1763 text entitled, *Der einzig mögliche Beweisgrund zu einer Demonstration des Daseins Gottes,* at the moment he attempts a positive articulation of the meaning of existence, Kant's voice trembles. There the nature of *Dasein* is determined at first by a distinction between the simple *Position* of a thing and that which is posited [*gesetzt*] in relation to some other thing. Kant writes: "Existence is the absolute position [*Position*] of the thing and thus is distinguished from every predicate which as such is always posited [*gesetzt wird*] merely with respect to some other thing."[8] Immediately, however, Kant seems to collapse the distinction: "The concept of *Position* or *Setzung* is totally simple and on the whole identical with the concept of being in general."[9] Here, Kant's voice can be heard to tremble; for the *difference* between *Position* and *Setzung* is elided by a disjunction that identifies the two. This disjunctive conjunction voices the trace of what Reiner Schürmann calls a "double comprehension of being" in Kant.[10]

Schürmann's engagements with Kant, both in his 1984 essay *Legislation-Transgression: Strategies and Counter-strategies in the Transcendental Justification of Norms* and in his magnum opus,

---

8   Immanuel Kant, *Kant's Gesammelte Schriften (Akademie-Ausgabe)* (Berlin: G. Reimer, 1902), II.73. Hereafter, *AA*.
9   Ibid.
10 Reiner Schürmann, *Broken Hegemonies,* trans. Reginald Lilly (Bloomington: Indiana University Press, 2003), 483.

Broken Hegemonies, are guided throughout by an attentive reading of the dynamic play between *Position* and *Setzung* in Kant, a play of language that is said to articulate two senses of being that shatter the autonomy of the transcendental subject, rendering it incapable of serving as the ultimate principle of legislative authority. In the complex and dynamic ways *Position* and *Setzung* are said in Kant, Schürmann discerns a tension between two senses of being that can be initially stated as follows: on the one hand, being is one of the categories through which the understanding gives rise to objects of possible experience; on the other hand, being is understood in a "pre-categorial" sense as pure givenness as such. Drawing on a remark Kant makes in the *Critique of Judgment* in which the term *Position* is used to designate "the representation of a thing with respect to our concept" and *Setzung* is used to point to the "thing in itself (apart from this concept)," Schürmann seeks to map these terms onto Kant's double comprehension of being by identifying *Position* with the thetic act that gives rise to existence as the second category of modality and *Setzung* with the pre-categorial apprehension of being as givenness.[11]

This terminological distinction, however, as Schürmann himself recognizes, vacillates as Kant's thinking shifts under the pressure of the Copernican turn in which the age old ontological question "What is being?" is at first subverted by the transcendental step back to the conditions for the possibility of *experience*, only then, in the second edition of the *Critique of Pure Reason*, to return with a vengeance that threatens to shatter the ultimate autonomy and thus authority of the transcendental

---

11 For the passage from the *Critique of Judgment*, see Immanuel Kant, *Kritik der Urteilskraft* (Hamburg: Felix Meiner Verlag, 1990), §76, 340. For Schürmann's attempt to map these terms onto the distinction between categorial and pre-categorial being, see Schürmann, *Broken Hegemonies*, 483. There Schürmann opts to translate *Position* as "thesis," and *Setzung* as "position." In what follows, however, the German terms are simply retained so that the difference to which they give voice may be more easily discerned and tracked in Kant.

subject.[12] By attending carefully to the manner in which the dual comprehension of being comes to language in Kant, Schürmann is able to discern the tragic truth the Kantian critical project must deny if it is to succeed. Schürmann puts it this way:

> Subjective spontaneity *turns received being against thetic being*. This is how the Kantian gesture that succeeds in instituting the modern referent remains, despite everything, faithful to the tragic truth, the truth of the conflict between the ultimates that have hold of us without recourse. Kant thematizes these as the impulse (of natality) toward autonomy, and then again as the impulse (of mortality) toward heteronomy. The first leads us to legislate universally. The second always returns us to the singular that occurs and is given outside of the universal, categorical law that the understanding declares. The differend between the conflictual strategies of being will turn transcendental logic into a broken imperative ontology.[13]

Kant's faithfulness to the tragic truth is only uncovered by a reading vigilantly attentive to what shows itself in language. Thus, even if, as this passage intimates and as Schürmann argues elsewhere, language is situated on the side of natality, autonomy, the universal, and the categorial, it nevertheless remains capable of articulating something of mortality, heteronomy, the singular, and givenness as such. The very trembling of language gestures to this capacity. Language can thus be heard to speak differently

---

12 Schürmann suggests, contrary to Heidegger in *Kant and the Problem of Metaphysics*, that the revisions Kant made to the *Critique of Pure Reason* between its first and second edition, when read with a view not exclusively toward the imagination, but through an examination of Kant's statements concerning being, mark not a retreat from the temporal understanding of being, but a decisive step toward the other, non-categorial sense of being as givenness that threatens to undermine the ultimate authority of transcendental self-consciousness. See Schürmann, *Broken Hegemonies*, 482. Cf. Martin Heidegger, *Kant and the Problem of Metaphysics*, trans. Richard Taft (Bloomington: Indiana University Press, 1990), §31, 110ff.

13 Schürmann, *Broken Hegemonies*, 483.

in those palpable moments when it encounters something of that which escapes its own subsumptive strategies.

An Other Language

Schürmann often identifies the subsumptive violence of predication with language and associates its universalizing function with the ontological trait of natality. Thus, he writes: "Fantasms install themselves as universals — thetic work proclaims them to be so, a work that is always accomplished by language."[14] For Schürmann, this is the linguistic work of natality on which life itself, "nourished on common significations," depends:[15] "we are lodged under the violence of the common, outside of which ... there is no life."[16] The entire project of *Broken Hegemonies* can be understood as an attempt to expose the hegemonic fantasms under which each linguistic epoch wins a life for itself by maximizing the thetic reality it posits as ultimate, even as it denies its own collusion in this thetic maximization. Schürmann puts it this way:

> A fantasm is hegemonic when an entire culture relies on it as if it provided that in the name of which one speaks and acts. Such a chief-represented (*hêgemôn*) is at work upon the unspeakable singular when it calls it a part of the whole; hegemonies transform the singular into a particular.[17]

---

14 Ibid., 44. Schürmann understands conceptual thought as parasitic on language. He insists, for example, that "no thought, however, has ever resisted being carried away by its own language. Far from mastering a language, concepts live on it: they are born of words." See ibid., 4. That language does not dissolve into concepts means that it is capable of expressing more than the merely conceptual.
15 Schürmann, *Broken Hegemonies*, 17.
16 Ibid., 22. See also 345: "Thus to the extent that, to live, it is necessary to speak and act, to understand and think, we will never extricate ourselves from poses and positions assumed, from theses put forth, and stops that are posited.... We will never extricate ourselves from legislative maximizings."
17 Ibid., 7.

Although the language of each epoch gives rise to its particular fantasm — ancient Greek posits the hegemony of the *hen*, medieval Latin that of *natura*, and modern German the hegemony of *Selbstbewußtsein* — the logic of ultimate referentiality remains fundamentally consistent: it is predicated on effacing the complex and dynamic encounter with the singular from which the hegemonic principle itself is born.

Yet Schürmann does not oppose the positing of hegemonic principles by means of a determinate negation that would remain bound to the same thetic act by which the law is instituted.[18] Rather, through an "analytic of ultimates,"[19] he exposes the denial inherent in the institution of the very principles that make a common life possible. Schürmann deploys a topological methodology that seeks to uncover the place of this denial, the site at which the thetic thrust of natality encounters and attempts to camouflage the dispersive counter-thrust of mortality: "Topology seeks to go back to the given, under the posited."[20] This topological analytic of ultimates, however, does not permit natality, the orginary archic trait that "prompts us toward new commencements and sovereign commandments," to pair off with mortality, the originary dispersive trait that "wrests us from the world of such archic referents."[21] Natality and mortality

---

18 Ibid., 622. Schürmann here insists upon a distinction between negation (*Verneinung*) and denial (*Verleugnung*): "Negating norms is a metaphysical operation that depends on a prior thetic act. On the other hand, denying a knowledge involves no such precursory normative thesis." Drawing on this distinction, he goes on to establish the difference between "destitution," which describes a fantasm that has lost its force of law, and "diremption," which "signifies the loss of every hegemony." See ibid., 623. The vocabulary of "diremption" must here be heard together with that of "discordance" suggested in chapter 1 and developed further in relation to the nuptial.
19 Schürmann, *Broken Hegemonies*, 6–7, 9.
20 Ibid., 348. For an excellent account of Schürmann's topological analytic of ultimates, see Reginald Lilly, "The Topology of *Des Hégémonies brisées*," *Research in Phenomenology* 28 (1998): 226–42, at 230–38.
21 Schürmann, *Broken Hegemonies*, 624. For another poignant formulation: "Once again, a summary of these pages would not be wrong in seeing in them a testing of a suspicion, namely, that the other of life does not fit in well with it; that their discord has always been known to us, however con-

do not consolidate into a unified system of oppositions — theirs is a nuptial union.

However, Schürmann himself articulates these originary traits in oppositional terms, associating natality on the one hand with the universal, the conceptual, and the violence of language, and mortality, on the other hand, with the singular, the given, and an ineluctable silence.[22] Nevertheless, the way the topological analytic of ultimates is performed in *Broken Hegemonies* opens a space for a different understanding of language in its relation to natality and mortality, one that Schürmann deploys but hardly thematizes. This other language is not subsumptive and apodictic, but rather attentive and apophantic. By attending to those moments of disruption expressed in and through language itself, something other than the subsumptive violence against the singular *is shown* to be at work in language. As we heard in our reading of Plotinus, the apophantic dimensions of language, its capacity to articulate phenomena as they show themselves to be, animates Schürmann's topological analytic of ultimates, turning it into a phenomenology of epochal *logoi*. Here is heard a kind of "legomenology," in which the things said in a given epoch themselves are taken as phenomenological clues to the originary denial upon which the ultimate referent of an epoch depends.[23]

---

fusedly; that death joins life without, however, forming a tandem with it, that it does not reflect life symmetrically nor oppose it with a determinate negation." See ibid., 23.

22 Such oppositions are posited and denied in the General Introduction to *Broken Hegemonies*, see specifically, Schürmann, *Broken Hegemonies*, 18–36.

23 The term "legomenology" grows out of a reading of Aristotle that emphasizes the manner in which he takes the things said, *ta legomena*, themselves as phenomena that lend insight into the nature of things. For a detailed discussion of this dimension of Aristotle's thinking, see Christopher P. Long, "Saving *Ta Legomena*: Aristotle and the History of Philosophy," *The Review of Metaphysics* 60, no. 2 (2006): 247–67. The term appears in print for the first time in Long, "The Daughters of Metis," 68. It is developed in more detail in Christopher P. Long, *Aristotle on the Nature of Truth* (New York: Cambridge University Press, 2011).

Schürmann attends carefully to the language by which the professional philosophers of each epoch, functioning as what Husserl called "civil servants of humanity," institute and legitimize hegemonic fantasms.[24] In so doing, however, he uncovers the language of the differend — the very articulation of that irreconcilable legislative conflict between two legitimate laws whereby the sovereignty of one necessarily involves the subversion of the other.[25] The language of the differend gives voice to an unstable community of relation between natality and mortality that conditions human existence. It is heard in the poetic language of tragedy that refuses to endure denial in silence, but attempts to bring the conflict of ultimates itself to language. Despite his own deep skepticism about philosophical language,

---

24 Schürmann appeals to Husserl's statement in the *Krisis* in order to indict professional philosophers for their collusion in the uncritical nomothetic legislation of hegemonic fantasms. See Edmund Husserl, *Die Krisis der europäischen Wissenschafen und die transzendentale Phänomenologie* (The Hague: Martinus Nijhoff, 1954), 15. Rodolphe Gasché, drawing on Schürmann's insistence that to understand a philosopher, one must seek the initial experience that "roused him to think" (*Broken Hegemonies*, 13), suggests that perhaps Schürmann's own thinking was guided by and remained concerned throughout with his experience with professional philosophers in the United States who were unwilling to turn their philosophical focus on the extent to which they too collude in the institution and legitimation of absolute ultimates. See Rodolphe Gasché, "Hegemonic Fantasms," *Research in Phenomenology* 35 (2005): 311–26, at 312.

25 Schürmann says that "the differend, in its place of emergence, expresses a conflict between the thesis of the same and the non-thetic other, the conflict of ultimates." See Schürmann, *Broken Hegemonies*, 32. Jean-François Lyotard puts the meaning of the differend this way: "As distinguished from a litigation, a differend [*différend*] would be a case of conflict, between (at least) two parties, that cannot be equitably resolved for lack of a rule of judgment applicable to both arguments. One side's legitimacy does not imply the other's lack of legitimacy. However, applying a single rule of judgment to both in order to settle their differend as though it were merely a litigation would wrong (at least) one of them (and both of them if neither side admits this rule)." See Jean-François Lyotard, *The Differend: Phrases in Dispute*, trans. Georges Van Den Abbeele (Minneapolis: University of Minnesota Press, 1988), xi. Schürmann uses the term to name the site where the singular that refuses particularization comes into conflict with the universal that seeks to set things in order.

Schürmann teaches philosophy the poetic language of tragedy and in so doing, rehabilitates a philosophical thinking capable of a kind of "tragic knowledge" that refuses to collude in the delusion endemic to its own legislative tendencies.[26] Indeed, Schürmann insists that "the differend is *articulated* in legislative-transgressive strategies that provide mortals with their condition of being, a broken condition that philosophers — those who know how to read — have never ceased to watch over."[27] In his careful, provocative and sometimes fantastic readings, Schürmann *articulates* the differend that shows itself each time a law is posited as ultimate.

Kant and the Transcendental Delusion

Kant offers a singularly perspicuous site for an investigation into the way the differend between the singular given and the legislating impulse come to language; for Kant is the master legislator who, in decisively establishing the autonomy of self-consciousness as the hegemonic fantasm of the modern age, unwittingly gives voice to "the unsubsumable other against which spontaneity collides."[28] Schürmann articulates Kant's peculiar relation to the tragic double bind this way:

> With full clarity, he sees a certain originary break through which the critical turn puts us, in the final instance, in a dou-

---

26 Schürmann, *Broken Hegemonies*, 622.
27 Ibid., 34, my emphasis. Gasché puts this point beautifully when he writes: "This critique of philosophy is not separable from its apology. *Broken Hegemonies* is the extraordinary document of a philosophical thought in conflict with itself — of philosophical thought thinking against itself in the name of philosophical thinking." See Gasché, "Hegemonic Fantasms," 312.
28 Schürmann, *Broken Hegemonies*, 484. Schürmann's account of the institution of the modern fantasm of self-consciousness begins with Luther, who "recognized, circumscribed, and resolutely occupied the site upon which every thought process and every conceptual strategy of the next four centuries were to work." See ibid., 353. Despite this bold claim, Schürmann unequivocally locates the *institution* of the modern fantasm of self-consciousness in Kant. See ibid., 355.

ble bind. He then evades the pathetic condition he perceived and escapes to the terrains adjacent to the transcendental, at times the terrain of the thing-in-itself, at others the terrain of appearance. It will be necessary to ask oneself if, here again, Kant has not recognized, and then denied, an originary *pathein,* a suffering which affects transcendental being.[29]

Schürmann pursues Kant's pathology of legislation first by exposing what he calls the "torments of autonomy," in which the autonomy of the transcendental subject is shown to be fractured at its core by "two incommensurable strategies within the same originarily transcendental freedom."[30] The one, associated with the transcendental *self,* names the very spontaneity that serves as the condition for possible experience. This is constitutive freedom, the autonomy that posits the very laws that condition all cognition and action. The other conception of freedom, associated with the *ego,* does not of necessity conform to the rational will — it points to a willfulness deprived of rules.[31] Schürmann describes the ego "as the inextirpable tendency to introduce the other, as a motive and means, right into the heart of reason."[32] The very possibility of moral action is itself predicated on an arbitrary will, pulled by impulses and desires, by "the murmur of alien, singular, solicitations," yet capable of freely choosing to conform to the moral law or of consciously embracing radical evil by subordinating itself to the motives of desire and legislating such subordinations as maxims.[33] The autonomy of the

---

29 Schürmann, *Broken Hegemonies,* 483.
30 Ibid., 480.
31 Ibid., 469, 480.
32 Ibid., 473.
33 Ibid., 471. Schürmann points to the discussion of radical evil in *Die Religion innerhalb der Grenzen der bloßen Vernunft* in which Kant identifies three human predispositions — 1) to animality, as living 2) to humanity, as living and rational, and 3) to personality as rational and accountable — all of which are said to "relate immediately to the ability to desire and the exercise of the arbitrary will [*Willkür*]." See Kant, *AA,* VI.26–8. Schürmann focuses on the fact that Kant does not trace evil back to self-love, but locates its root in the relation between the rational will and the arbitrary will. This is where

transcendental self expresses the trait of natality, the autonomy of the ego that of mortality. Taken together, they point to the site of a ineluctable fissure in the attempt to ground cognitive, ethical, and pragmatic legislation on the autonomy of the subject.

Yet Schürmann's reading of the torments of the autonomy of self-consciousness is in fact already informed by the suspicion that there is a deeper, more originary fissure at the core of Kant's thinking, a rupture over against which these torments, however disquieting, appear as mere symptoms. This suspicion is most clearly articulated in Schürmann's introduction to Part Three of *Broken Hegemonies*, entitled "In the Name of Consciousness: The Modern Hegemonic Fantasm." There he writes:

> Following the thread of an entirely coherent concatenation of arguments (even though it has escaped the attention of most commentators) from the precritical writings up to the *Critique of Judgment*, we will see that a conflict between two senses of being splits self-consciousness; that the referent from which the moderns expect supreme legislation produces, simultaneously and necessarily, its own transgression....[34]

Kant "introduces heteronomy right into the general function of reason." See Schürmann, *Broken Hegemonies*, 472. For his part, Kant says: "The wickedness (*vitiosita, pravitas*) or, if you like, the corruption (*corruptio*) of the human heart is the tendency of the arbitrary will to maxims which neglect the incentives arising from the moral law in favor of others (that are not moral)." See Kant, *AA*, VI.30.

34 Schürmann, *Broken Hegemonies*, 355. Of course, one commentator who decidedly did not allow this ontological distinction to escape his attention is Heidegger. Schürmann seems to borrow heavily from some of the core insights of Heidegger's "Kants These über das Sein," although he nowhere cites this essay in his discussion of Kant. Nevertheless, it is Heidegger who identifies the meaning of being for Kant as positing and who first maps out the contours of the itinerary Schürmann will follow. Heidegger traces Kant's thesis concerning being from the pre-critical 1763 text on the proof of God's existence to the *Critique of Pure Reason* where the thesis that being is positing finds bold expression in the text on the *Impossibility of an Ontological Proof and in the Postulates of Empirical Thought in General*. He then gestures to section 76 of the Critique of Judgment, where, he says, "in order for the object to be cognized as actual, it requires affection from the senses." See Martin Heidegger, "Kants These über das Sein," in *Wegmarken*

To follow the thread of this argument, however, uncovers the manner in which the differend at work in all nomothetic legislation shows itself in language.

The first intimation of this originary conflict between two senses of being in Kant has already been heard in the pre-critical, 1763 *Beweisgrund* text. There Kant's voice trembles as he first articulates a difference between *Position* and the sort of *Setzung* associated with predication only then immediately to identify the two.[35] Strangely enough, Schürmann does not point to this passage in the text, but rather to two other passages in which, he argues, the vocabulary of *Setzung* refers unequivocally to an originary givenness that precedes the thetic activity of the subject. Before turning to these specific passages, however, it is important to recognize that at least in the initial articulation of the meaning of *Position* in the *Beweisgrund* text, the cognate of *Setzung* refers not to originary givenness, but to those relations of predication by which something is posited [*gesetzt wird*] with respect to something else. Such predications are closely associated with the relation things have to their properties over against which Kant wants to distinguish the simple concept of

---

(Frankfurt am Main: Vittorio Klostermann, 1976), 470. Finally, Heidegger returns to the *Amphiboly of Concepts of Reflection in the Critique of Pure Reason* to trace a new step in Kant's interpretation of being, a step that involves the "reflection on reflection" where being as positing is fit into the structure of human subjectivity. For an interesting discussion of this aspect of Heidegger's reading of Kant, see Avery Goldman, "The Metaphysics of Kantian Epistemology," *Proceedings of the American Catholic Philosophical Association* 76 (2002): 239–52. Goldman shows there the manner in which Heidegger's approach to Kant in the "Kants These über das Sein" is designed to show the presuppositions that underwrite the critical project itself. To this extent, Heidegger's and Schürmann's projects dovetail, for Schürmann's attempt to articulate an understanding of being as pure givenness is itself a way of uncovering the irreducible condition for the possibility of the critical project itself, a condition covered over by tragic denial. A comparative interpretation of Heidegger and Schürmann's reading of section 76 of the *Critique of Judgment* would illustrate how Heidegger holds firm to sensibility as the prior source of the critical project, while Schürmann identifies a givenness that precedes sensibility as the ineluctable condition the critical project must deny if it is to succeed.

35 Kant, *AA*, II.73.

Position.³⁶ By collapsing the difference between *Position* and *Setzung* here, Kant already implicitly opens the space for an another understanding of *Setzung*, one that extends beyond the positing endemic to predication.³⁷

Schürmann locates precisely such a pre-predicative apprehension of *Setzung* in Kant's discussion of possibility in the 1763 text. There Kant considers the formal conditions under which possibility itself is possible. He distinguishes between logical impossibility, which simply involves internal contradiction, and the vanishing of possibility which happens "when no matter or no datum is there to think."³⁸ This allows Kant first to suggest the following: "If, then, all existence is denied, then nothing whatsoever is posited [*so ist nichts schlechthin gesetzt*], nothing at all is given [*gegeben*], no matter of anything to be thought upon, and all possibility vanishes entirely."³⁹ Here, Kant seems to suggest: *nichts gesetzt, nichts gegeben,* nothing posited, nothing given; and when nothing is given, nothing can be thought and possibility itself disappears. Kant goes on to argue: "That there be some possibility and yet absolutely nothing actual, contradicts itself; for, if nothing exists, also nothing is given which would be thinkable there, and one would contradict oneself if

---

36 Jaakko Hintikka suggests that Kant introduces the term setzen here and in the analogous passage from the *Critique of Pure Reason*, A598/B626, because he has "a desire to have a term which sits more happily with the cases in which 'is' apparently has a merely predicative function." See Jaakko Hintikka, "Kant on Existence, Predication, and the Ontological Argument," in *The Logic of Being: Historical Studies* (Dordrecht: D. Reidel, 1986), 257.

37 Although Hintikka finds a distinction between absolute and relative positing expressed in the *Beweisgrund* text, he insists that "Kant clearly thinks of the 'is' of predication (the copula) and the 'is' of existence as two uses of the same notion." Using the Frege-Russell thesis that 'is' is ambiguous in multiple ways, Hintikka maps the notion of relative positing in Kant, that is, positing something in relation to something, onto the "is" of predication; absolute positing, on the other hand, seems to map onto the "is" of existence. Yet, Hintikka thinks these two different senses of 'is' are not held distinct in Kant. See ibid., 258–59.

38 Kant, *AA*, II.78.

39 Ibid., II.78.

one nevertheless pretends that something is possible."[40] Drawing on these two sentences, Schürmann generates a poignant equation to illustrate how Kant consolidates the meaning of *Setzung* by identifying it first with the "given" and then by extending the meaning of the given to existence. Thus, Schürmann writes: "*Setzung = Gegebensein = Dasein.*"[41]

The articulation of *Setzung* in the pre-critical 1763 text is thus said to gesture to an understanding of being that precedes the thetic activity of the subject. Schürmann himself identifies the relation between saying and being expressed here with Aristotelian logic, "where ways of saying reflect, without thereby creating a problem, ways of being."[42] Schürmann's own topological analytic of ultimates itself trades on something like the Aristotelian recognition that the ways things are said express something of the truth of being. Thus, by attending carefully to the way "positing" is said in Kant, Schürmann is able to uncover a pre-categorial apprehension of being at work in the 1763 *Beweisgrund* text. This other, non-thetic sense of positing and with it the sense of being as givenness is then pursued into the text of the *Critique of Pure Reason* where, under the pressure of the Copernican turn, there appears a "terminological chiasmus" between *Position* and *Setzung* that articulates the shifting ontological ground on which the transcendental project depends.[43] In turning to the thetic activity of the transcendental subject in order to secure the conditions for the possibility of experience, Kant trades on and yet covers over the originary sense of being as extrinsic givenness, thus rendering all givenness intrinsic under the subjective conditions of sensibility.[44] Yet, for Schür-

---

40 Ibid., II.78.
41 Schürmann, *Broken Hegemonies*, 486.
42 Ibid.
43 Ibid., 672.
44 According to Schürmann, Kant trades on the originary sense of being insofar as he insists that the critical project presupposes, not merely a negative, but also a positive conception of the noumenon. This positive conception of the noumenon is heard in the preface to the second edition of the *Critique of Pure Reason*, where Kant insists upon the difference between cognition and thinking in order to open the space by which to *think* things in themselves.

mann, the Copernican turn, however radical, "cannot disown a certain understanding of being."[45] The sense of being as extrinsic givenness and articulated in the 1763 text by cognates of *Setzung*, remains operative in the *Critique of Pure Reason*, although there *Position* rather than *Setzung* expresses the pre-categorial sense of being as givenness.

Schürmann locates this terminological chiasmus in two texts from the 1787 second edition of the *Critique of Pure Reason* where *Setzung* and its cognates come to designate the categorial sense of being that results from the positing activity of the mind, whereas *Position* is said to gesture to extra-mental being as givenness. First, in the discussion of sensibility in the *Transcendental Aesthetic*, Kant repeatedly deploys the cognates of *setzen* to designate the manner in which the mind affects itself by its own capacity for sensible intuition. Thus, Kant writes:

> Now that which, as representation, can precede any act of thinking something is intuition and, if it contains nothing but relations, it is the form of intuition, which, since it does not represent anything except insofar as something is posited [*gesetzt*] in the mind, can be nothing other than the way in which the mind is affected by its own activity, namely this positing [*dieses Setzen*] of its representation, thus the way it is affected through itself....[46]

If this were not possible, Kant says, "there would follow the absurd proposition that there is an appearance without anything that appears." See Immanuel Kant, *Kritik der reinen Vernunft* (Hamburg: Meiner Verlag, 1990), Bxxvi–xxvii. This appeal to appearance, Schürmann suggests, covers over the irreducible sense of being as givenness: "The force of the denial is obvious in the sleight of hand played upon appearance. From the pure event of appearing (in the infinitive sense), it is reified into that which appears (in the nominative sense)." See Schürmann, *Broken Hegemonies*, 492.

45 Reiner Schürmann, "Legislation-Transgression: Strategies and Counter-Strategies in the Transcendental Justification of Norms," *Man and World* 17 (1984): 361–98, at 372.
46 Kant, *Kritik der reinen Vernunft*, B67–68.

Here, *gesetzt* and *setzen* articulate the self-affective activity of the mind. They point not to being as pure givenness, but to the mind's receptive capacity under the subjective condition of sensibility. The repetition of cognates of *Setzung* in this passage expresses intrinsic rather than extrinsic givenness.[47] The Copernican turn has thus turned the meaning of *Setzung*. Although it retains here a sense of givenness, it no longer points to the pre-categorial givenness of being, but to the self-affective activity of the mind by which it gives itself representations. Indeed, if the transcendental project is to succeed in uncovering the *a priori* conditions for the possibility of experience, it must deny the very possibility of a givenness outside the purview of the self-affective activity of the subject.

Yet Schürmann's analysis exposes this denial by attending to the decussating senses of *Setzung* in order to articulate a tension in the meaning of givenness Kant somehow recognizes but nevertheless leaves shrouded. Thus, in a poignant moment at the end of the first step of the transcendental deduction, in which Kant attempts to abstract from sensibility in order to uncover the conditions for the possibility of the understanding,[48] he admits the following:

> In the above proof, however, I still could not abstract from one point, namely, from the fact that the manifold for intu-

---

47 Reading the rest of this passage (B67ff), Schürmann recognizes that "in the space of ten lines, the verb *setzen* occurs there five times. It designates (1) the intuition in internal sense as the investment (*besetzen,* ibid.) of that sense with relations; (2) an act concerning, not the thing in itself, but representation in its temporality ('*die Zeit, in die* [sic] *wir diese Vorstellungen setzen*'); (3) affection not through extrinsic givenness, but intrinsic givenness; time is that through which the mind affects itself ('*die Art, wie das Gemüt durch eigene Tätigkeit, nämlich dieses Setzen seiner Vorstellung, mithin durch sich self affiziert wird*')." See Schürmann, *Broken Hegemonies,* 672n154.

48 For a discussion of the manner in which the deduction proceeds by two-steps, see Christopher P. Long, "Two Powers, One Ability: The Understanding and Imagination in Kant's Critical Philosophy," *The Southern Journal of Philosophy* 36, no. 2 (1998): 233–53, at 234–36. See also Dieter Henrich, "The Proof Structure of Kant's Transcendental Deduction," *Review of Metaphysics* 22, no. 4 (1969): 640–59.

ition must already be *given* prior to the synthesis of understanding and independently from it; how, however, is here left undetermined.[49]

Schürmann reads this as a gesture to another sense of givenness, one that is intimated only to be left undetermined. The question as to how what is given in intuition is itself given to intuition remains inaccessible. And yet, in the shifting meaning of *Setzung* something of an originary givenness, of an irreducible suffering, comes to language. Schürmann puts it this way: "These problems are knotted together in affection. It is in affection that position [i.e., *Setzung*] now turns aside from givenness and that makes the regime tremble."[50]

Yet, even in the *Critique of Pure Reason*, where *Setzung* and its cognates articulate the manner in which all givenness must run necessarily through the subjective conditions of sensibility, another sort of givenness comes to language in a second text to which Schürmann appeals as he attempts to hear in the vacillating meaning of *Position* and *Setzung* a denial of the meaning of being as givenness. In the section entitled "On the Impossibility of an Ontological Proof of God's Existence," Kant famously claims: "Being is obviously not a real predicate, i.e., a concept of something that could add to the concept of a thing. It is merely the Position of a thing or of certain determinations in themselves."[51] In a footnote to his 1984 text on legislation that anticipates the deeper reading of Kant pursued in *Broken Hegemonies,* Schürmann appeals to these famous Kantian sentences in order to insist: "'Positing' does not mean here the self-instituting of a supreme ground but the fact that in experience something is being experienced. Positedness means facticity. It enters language through the copula."[52] Schürmann thus reads the term *Position* in Kant's discussion of the ontological proof

---

49 Kant, *Kritik der reinen Vernunft*, B145.
50 Schürmann, *Broken Hegemonies*, 488. Recall that Schürmann translates *Setzung* as "position." See ibid., 483.
51 Kant, *Kritik der reinen Vernunft*, B626.
52 Schürmann, "Legislation-Transgression," 394.

in the *Critique of Pure Reason* as gesturing to extrinsic being as pure givenness that precedes all operations of the transcendental mind.[53] *Position* names here what *Setzung* named in the 1763 text: the extrinsic givenness of being. Even here, however, a strict terminological distinction does not hold, for in analyzing the sentence "God is omnipotent," Kant insists that it contains two concepts, God and omnipotence, while "the little word 'is' is not a predicate in it, but rather only that which posits [*setzt*] the predicate in relation to the subject."[54] If positedness means facticity here and comes to language through the copula, it does not settle squarely into the terminological distinction between *Position* and *Setzung,* for both terms seem ambiguously capable of pointing to the categorial and pre-categorial senses of being. Kant's language here again trembles. Schürmann himself insists that no definite terminological distinction between *Position* and *Setzung* is established until, in the *Critique of Judgment,* Kant returns to the question of the possible in relation to the actual in order to claim that

> the former [namely, the actual] signifies only the *Position* of the representation of a thing with respect to our concept and, in general, our faculty for thinking, while the later [namely, the actual] signifies the *Setzung* of the thing in itself (apart from this concept).[55]

Here the terminological grounds have shifted again, and *Position* names categorial, intrinsic being, while *Setzung* names extra-mental being as givenness apart from the concept.

In this articulation of *Setzung,* which is said to point here to an actuality outside the concept, Schürmann hears the echo of an originary suffering on which all transcendental positing depends. He writes:

---

53 Schürmann, *Broken Hegemonies,* 672.
54 Kant, *Kritik der reinen Vernunft,* B626–27.
55 Kant, *Kritik der Urteilskraft,* 336.

> *Position* emphasizes, then, the relation of a conceived representation to the understanding, and hence, the possible; *Setzung* emphasizes the relation to sensibility of the material one suffers, and hence the actual. Thus the singular is recognized in its contingency and randomness ....[56]

Attending to the ambiguity of being voiced in the ambiguity of language at play in the various senses of *Position* and *Setzung*, Schürmann brings the agony of Kantian theticism to language, thus giving voice to the "pathetic condition of being" Kant is said to have "seen clearly" and insistently denied.[57]

The Logic of Denial

If in the *Critique of Pure Reason*, the ambiguous play of *Position* and *Setzung* gives voice to the manner in which an obstreperous givenness, despite all evasion, intrudes upon transcendental self-consciousness from without, the fundamental yet enigmatic distinction between the I-think and the I-am in Kant exposes transcendental self-consciousness to singularity from within. Schürmann traces the logic of Kantian denial to the site of this distinction. A brief account of the play between the I-think and the I-am in Kant articulates a tension that must be denied if the transcendental subject's ultimate legislative authority is to be secured. In articulating the manner in which singularity at once intrudes upon the subject from without and shatters it from within, Schürmann's reading of Kant allows us to discern another language of natality, one that is not simply subsumptive in nature, but also capable of bringing to expression a kind of tragic knowledge, indeed, a nuptial responsibility, vigilantly attuned to the violence of its own operation.

Toward the end of the transcendental deduction, in §25, Kant returns to the original synthetic unity of apperception in which, he says, "I am conscious to myself not as I appear to myself, nor

---

56 Schürmann, *Broken Hegemonies*, 506.
57 Ibid., 485 and 95–96.

as I am in myself, but only that I am. This representation is a *thinking*, not an *intuiting*."⁵⁸ According to Schürmann, this simple awareness *that I am* cleaves heart of transcendental spontaneity.⁵⁹ This can be heard in an enigmatic and poignant note found in the middle of §25 in which Kant writes:

> The *I think* expresses the act [*Actus*] of determining my existence. The existence is thereby already given, but the way in which I am to determine it, i.e., the manifold that I am to posit in myself [*in mir setzen solle*], is not yet thereby given.⁶⁰

Here the term *setzen* remains firmly situated within the transcendental apparatus insofar as it is associated with the way the mind gives itself the intuitions according to which something may be cognized. Yet Kant here seems to open the space in which to think an existence apart from what is given in intuition, that is, apart from the transcendental conditions under which experience first becomes possible. This existence is the simple awareness that I-am, itself neither noumenal nor phenomenal.⁶¹ This awareness of the I-am seems to escape the productive powers of the transcendental subject, and yet, there it is. The other strategies of evasion Kant deploys to cover over this sort of insistent givenness — to declare it noumenal and thus outside scope of the transcendental project or to crush it under the thetic regime of subjective spontaneity — remain unavailable, for in the I-am, an irreducible awareness of my own singularity announces it-

---

58 Kant, *Kritik der reinen Vernunft*, B157.
59 Schürmann, *Broken Hegemonies*, 496.
60 Kant, *Kritik der reinen Vernunft*, B157.
61 Schürmann appeals to a note in the Paralogisms section of the Doctrine of Elements in which Kant gestures to a heteronomous and fleeting sort of mental material that points to an existence that is neither an appearance nor a thing in itself. See Schürmann, *Broken Hegemonies*, 497. Kant there speaks of an indeterminate perception of "something real, which was given, and indeed only to thinking in general, thus not as appearance, and also not as a thing in itself (*noumenon*), but rather as something that in fact exists and is indicated as an existing thing in the proposition 'I think.'" See Kant, *Kritik der reinen Vernunft*, B423.

self. With the I-am, the I-think encounters itself as singular. Schürmann puts it this way: "if its nature is that it 'determines my existence,' then the I-think will have to be adjoined to an indeterminate givenness as equi-originary. The I-am *singularizes* the I-think, the universal legislator."[62]

Transcendental legislation shows itself here as pathological; for it remains conditioned by an irreducible givenness, a *pathos*, that at once escapes and makes possible the legislative spontaneity of the transcendental subject.[63] The subject is thus exposed to a suffering it did not make and cannot escape. According to Schürmann, Kant sees this "with full clarity," but then denies it: "The transcendental critique recognizes the other that places us at its mercy, but it denies it as soon as it recognizes it."[64] But Kant is no Agamemnon; for Agamemnon unequivocally recognizes the double bind in which he is situated. He says explicitly:

> Heavy is my fate if I do not obey, but heavy too, if I slaughter my daughter, delight of my house, by maiden sacrifice, staining these father's hands with rivers of blood beside the alter. What of these things is without evils?[65]

Kant's recognition is neither seen with such clarity nor voiced with such urgency. Schürmann himself admits that the tragic double bind that conditions the hegemonic fantasm of modernity is heard not so much in what Kant explicitly says, as in the vehemence by which the sense of being as givenness is denied.[66] Yet even this suggests perhaps too much, for the Kantian denial of singularity itself comes to language precisely as Kant so

---

62 Schürmann, *Broken Hegemonies*, 498.
63 Schürmann insists that the pathological should not be confused with the original pathos that names the irreducible suffering endemic to encounters with the singular. To call transcendental legislation "pathological" is to recognize it as bound to this originary suffering. To speak of the "pathology of being" is to articulate the pathos endemic to the manner in which being comes to language.
64 Schürmann, *Broken Hegemonies*, 504.
65 Aeschylus, Denniston, and Page, *Agamemnon*, ll. 206–11.
66 Schürmann, *Broken Hegemonies*, 505.

powerfully articulates the legislative thrust of transcendental subjectivity. The very positing of the ultimate authority of the subject brings the singular to language. Here, perhaps, we are not dealing with recognition and denial, but, to use the Freudian vocabulary, with a pre-conscious awareness of the conflict and its repression.[67] Freud develops his understanding of the unconscious from the theory of repression in which an idea that is, for whatever reason, repressed, remains both inaccessible to consciousness and yet effective.[68] Some such repressed ideas are said to be "unconscious" when they remain ultimately inaccessible to consciousness, having been kept from consciousness by continuing pressure, others, however, are said to be "preconscious" when, under certain conditions, they are capable of becoming conscious.[69] If these Freudian distinctions are mapped on to Schürmann's reading of Kant, perhaps it is possible to say that in the pre-critical writings and in the first edition of the *Critique of Pure Reason,* the sense of being as givenness and with it the irreducible encounter with singularity operate unconsciously in Kant. The repressed conflict between two senses of being is heard, however, in the way Kant's voice trembles as he articulates the nature of existence and its relation to positing. Thus, although the trace of that other sense of being as givenness comes to language here, it remains inaccessible to Kant. With the Copernican turn, however, and more specifically, with the second edition of the *Critique of Pure Reason,* where Schür-

---

67 Rodolphe Gasché has suggested that Schürmann's thinking, particularly his emphasis on the way in which "fantasms" operate hegemonically by obsessively maximizing a particular phenomenon or representation in a way that obscures all others, "suggests a psychoanalytic reading." See Gasché, "Hegemonic Fantasms," 313. It is doubtful that Schürmann himself would have embraced such a reading.

68 See Sigmund Freud, *The Standard Edition of the Complete Psychological Works of Sigmund Freud, Vol. 19: The Ego and the Id and Other Works,* trans. James Strachey in collaboration with Anna Freud (London: Hogarth Press, 1955), 15. See also Richard Wollheim, *Sigmund Freud* (New York: Viking Press, 1971), 176.

69 See Freud, *The Standard Edition,* XIX, 16. See also Wollheim, *Sigmund Freud,* 180.

mann insists that Kant took "a step forward, and a giant leap at that, toward an abyss traversing being itself," Kant encounters something irreducibly given that conditions the legislative authority of the subject but is not produced by it.[70] The sense of being as pure givenness threatens to undermine the entire critical project. It thus must be repressed by a continuous pressure that comes to language at certain critical moments — in the distinction between the I-think and the I-am, in the repetitive deployment of cognates of *Setzung* in describing the subjective conditions under which intuitions are given, and in the articulation of the meaning of existence as *Position* in the section dealing with the proof for the existence of God. Schürmann's topological legomenology itself brings these moments to language in such a way that they can no longer be denied to consciousness. Thus, Schürmann's analytic of ultimates here uncovers a preconscious awareness in Kant of an originary conflict that must be repressed if the legislative authority of the transcendental subject is to be securely established and legitimated. Translating psychoanalytic repression into the language of denial, Schürmann writes:

> Apart from sporadic assertions of the second edition of the *Critique of Pure Reason*, the givenness of the singular is only implied with the doctrinal meaning of being, for it is recognized only through the intensity of the denial, of the suppression, of the censure, of the endlessly striving theticism of triumphant, spontaneous autonomy.[71]

Yet by tracing the topology of this suppression, Schürmann brings to language a way of thinking that can no longer abide the repression of the originary conflict. In so doing, however, he practices a way of philosophical saying that is capable of criti-

---

70 Schürmann, *Broken Hegemonies*, 482.
71 Ibid., 505.

cally engaging the manner in which language colludes in the violence of the common on which life itself depends.[72]

The Voice of Singularity and the Philosophy-to-Come

Schürmann's topological legomenology models a way of thinking and performs a philosophical saying capable of doing a certain justice to the suffering of the singular. Here the genitive is both subjective and objective, the singular suffers and is suffered — the encounter with singularity upon which life depends always operates in the middle voice. This is the ambiguous voice of singularity, the tremor of mortality heard in and through the language of natality. Here the language of natality is heard to involve more than the violent imposition of the subject upon the object, the forceful suppression of the singular under universal predicates that render it particular. Rather, the apophantic dimensions of the language of natality itself brings to expression the voice of the singular, irreducible and insistent, that irrepressibly operates in all our attempts to speak and act together in meaningful ways.[73] If Schürmann names the condition that fractures every referent posited as ultimate *singularization to come,* associating it with the ontological trait of mortality, perhaps the thinking that remains assiduously attuned to the manner in which this fracture comes to language despite all at-

---

72 Ibid., 22.
73 At the very end of *Broken Hegemonies,* Schürmann gestures to the way of thinking and philosophical saying associated here with natality, but he segregates natality from this other thinking and saying: "The analytic of ultimates holds forth upon the hegemonic fantasms, but an epilogue to fantasms as such is literally unthinkable, just as it is unthinkable not to enlist universals into the service of some consoling and consolidating noun. All common nouns are capable of this, for we think and speak under the fantasmogenic impetus of natality. It is, however, possible to enlarge one's way of thinking beyond the fantasied common. In our languages, verbs in the middle voice always lead their speaker out of simple nominative lawmaking. It is, then, possible to think for itself the double bind that we know." See ibid., 631. Perhaps this requires the very imagination beyond the limits of thinking with which we began.

tempted repression could be associated with natality and called a *philosophy to come* in which the voice of singularity is heard to express an irreducible otherness that holds us accountable and opens us always to new possibilities for community.[74]

A *philosophy to come* would require an imagination beyond the limits of thinking attuned to "mortal natality" and its chiasmus, "natal mortality." "Mortal natality" names the manner in which natal habits of thinking, acting, and speaking not only refuse to cover over and repress the conditions of their own operation, but also open themselves to the possibilities that come to language at the site of the encounter with singularity. The mortality of natality thus would not forsake the common altogether, but would inject every attempt to enter into community with others with a dimension of openness that would render it inherently unstable and thus always in need of critical re-articulation. Yet if mortal natality names the condition under which a philosophy-to-come would need to relate itself critically to each gathering of community in which it finds itself embedded, natal mortality names the condition under which the singular, despite its ineffable unicity, comes nevertheless to language in a way that can be heard to hold all such critical re-articulations to account. "Natal mortality" points to the manner in which death itself refuses mute silence but continually comes to language with an urgency that can be neither repressed nor denied. Indeed, the natality of mortality infuses life with an insistent injunction to respond to the voice of singularity as the site of an ongoing, asymmetrical dialogue where new, more just, beginnings not only become possible, but insistently necessary.

* * *

If Agamemnon, voice trembling, consolidates his sovereign authority by turning a deaf ear to Iphigeneia at Aulis, Oedipus, eyes blind, relinquishes his by attending to the voice of Antigone

---

74 Schürmann writes, "Mortality familiarizes us with our singularization to come." See ibid., 19, 14.

as she leads him to Colonus. The *Oedipus at Colonus* begins with a question:

> Antigone, child of a blind man, to what
> region have we come, or to what city of which men?[75]

The place, they will soon discover, is the grove sacred to the Eumenides on the outskirts of Athens. This place connects the story of Oedipus topologically with that of Agamemnon. Each place has its history, and this sacred grove can be traced back to that original act of thetic violence Agamemnon perpetrated on his daughter at Aulis.

We might, indeed, trace a powerful symbolic reversal announced in these opening lines of *Oedipus at Colonus*. At Aulis, Agamemnon, destitute, commands the sacrifice that kills his daughter and secures his sovereignty. This violent denial contains within it the seeds of the destruction of Agamemnon's authority; for he will return from Troy only to be killed by Clytemnestra, who, in turn, will be killed by their son, Orestes, as the cycle of the politics of patriarchal retribution unfolds as it has for generations, and as it continues today, three millennia later. At Colonus, on the other hand, Oedipus, destitute, asks his daughter where they are, names her, and reaches out to her for support. This caring gesture contains within it the seeds of another politics. Its signature can be heard already in the shift from the imperative to the interrogative voice in the two texts. Where Agamemnon commands, Oedipus asks. The stories are deeply intertwined, for Antigone and Oedipus find themselves in the sacred grove of the Eumenides, the very goddesses, now transformed, who then pursued Orestes, seeking blood for the blood of his murdered mother, Clytemnestra. It was Athena, of course, who, seeking to secure peace in her city, honored the

---

75 Sophocles, *Sophoclis Fabulae*, OC, ll. 1–2.

Furies as sacred to Athens, if they would allow themselves to be persuaded to give up the destructive pursuit of vengeance.[76]

Thus, at the beginning of *Oedipus at Colonus* we find ourselves in a sacred space opened by a willingness to relinquish the retributive practices of patriarchal violence for a different, gentler, and therefore more audacious politics. Weaving these stories together, Sophocles invites us to consider the sort of community that is possible when the logic of patriarchal dominion withers.

---

[76] For a fuller account of the story and its broader political implications, see Long, "The Daughters of Metis."

5

A Politics of the Between

*I have the things I love most, death would no longer make
me all-wretched, with you two placed beside me.
Press close upon my ribs, children, on both sides…*
— Sophocles, *Oedipus at Colonus*, ll. 1110–12[1]

If, as we suggested at the end of chapter three — the middle panel of this triptych text — new constellations of meaning and thus new possibilities for community open through our responsive engagement with what is said in a text, perhaps an interpretation of the relationship that unfolds between Oedipus and his daughters in the grove sacred to the Eumenides can teach us something about the habits of nuptial response-ability that conditions the possibility of poetic politics. The political power of hermeneutical responsiveness is at the heart of what Schürmann calls "symbolic praxis," an invitation to action awakened by and attuned to the symbolic play between reader and text. Here, reading becomes political, interpretation practical.

If, indeed, our readings of Aristotle, Plotinus, and Kant have been effective, they will not simply have been convincing; rather, they will have opened us to new modes of being and acting capable of transforming our relationships with one another and the communities we inhabit. The effective power of sym-

---

[1] Sophocles, *Sophoclis Fabulae* (Oxford: Clarendon Press, 1990).

bolic praxis is at the root of poetic politics. A central teaching of Schürmann's work is that symbols, in acting upon us, set us into action: "Symbols...naturally give rise to a behavior. ... The *poietics* of the symbol gives one something to do. Symbols create."[2] Reiner Schürmann died too soon; but he left us texts that give us something to do. In tracing the contours of the ultimate principles that have established themselves, reigned, and withered through the history of western thinking and acting, *Broken Hegemonies* uncovers the ineluctable play of natality and mortality that conditions human existence. The book itself points to the ravaged site we must learn to inhabit if we are to enrich our ways of being together. This demonstrative gesture, however, not unlike the gesture Oedipus made in pointing out to Theseus the site of his death, invites us into to the question of how we together might effectively inhabit such a site ravaged by the chiasmic play of natality and mortality. Here too, Schürmann inscribed into the text of *Broken Hegemonies* itself signs that have now led us to the grove of the Eumenides at Colonus. In this, it has led us back to the place from which we began so we might make yet again a new beginning.

If, however, we allow the story of *Oedipus at Colonus* to resonate against that of Agamemnon and read it through the shattered history of patriarchal sovereignty to which *Broken Hegemonies* itself awakens us, we might discern the political significance of the tenuous, discordant, and yet eloquent relationship between Oedipus and his daughters as they seek to inhabit a ravaged site born of exile that offers no recourse beyond the ultimate play of natality and mortality. In bringing the contours of the relationships between Oedipus, Antigone, and Ismene to language, the Sophoclean text gives us something to do by demonstrating how it might be possible to enrich our communities even as we are ravaged by the monstrous site we inhabit together. The symbols endemic to these relationships point us to

---

2   Reiner Schürmann, "Symbolic Praxis," *The Graduate Faculty Philosophy Journal* 19/20, no. 2/1 (1997): 39–65, at 39.

the habits of nuptial response-ability we would need to cultivate to bring such a poetic politics to life.

Moments of Truth and Transformation

In tragedy as in life, moments of truth are transformative. Aristotle tells us that such moments are most beautiful when, as in *Oedipus Tyrannus,* the movement from ignorance to recognition is accompanied by a reversal that marks a change into the opposite of the things previously done.[3] Such moments of recognition and reversal open new possibilities for community by transforming the logic of relation that conditions human being-together. Yet, the possibilities that open at such moments of truth can dissolve as suddenly as they appear, for old habits reassert themselves, compelling the repetition of the very destructive modes of relation that led to crisis in the first place.[4]

Despite the cathartic effects of repeated reversals attended by recognition, human politics continues to reinscribe itself in delusional and self-destructive fantasies of hegemony. Principles are repeatedly posited as absolute only to wither over time, eroded by the denial endemic to their institution, as the play of natality and mortality inevitably compels us to recognize that the principles themselves are as finite and conditional as we are who posited them as ultimate in the beginning. And yet, to trace the possibilities of relation that open in those tragic moments of transformation, to draw out their contours and carefully consider the logic according to which they operate, is already to begin to learn something of what tragedy has to teach: a way of

---

[3] Aristotle and Rudolf Kassel. *Aristotelis De Arte Poetica Liber* (Oxonii: E Typographeo Clarendoniano, 1966), 1452a22–34.

[4] Freud identified this as a *Widerholungszwang,* or a repetition compulsion, in *Beyond the Pleasure Principle.* See Sigmund Freud, "Beyond the Pleasure Principle," in *The Standard Edition of the Complete Psychological Works of Sigmund Freud, Vol. 18: Beyond the Pleasure Principle, Group Psychology and Other Works,* trans. James Strachey in collaboration with Anna Freud (London: Hogarth Press, 1955). For a short but succinct discussion of repetition compulsion in Freud, see Jean Laplanche and J. B. Pontalis, *The Language of Psycho-Analysis,* 1st edn. (New York: W.W. Norton, 1974), 78–80.

human being-together rooted in the acute recognition of mortal finitude and interdependence.

This teaching is at the heart of Sophocles' *Oedipus at Colonus,* a drama written at the end of Sophocles' life and situated in the middle of a trilogy that begins with *Oedipus Tyrannus* and ends with *Antigone.* Whatever else these two latter plays are about, they also articulate the repetition compulsion endemic to archic politics and the self-destructive logic of hegemonic violence that is properly called patriarchal. Between these two tragic illustrations of the limits of patriarchal dominion, however, stands *Oedipus at Colonus,* a tragedy that offers a powerful image of the father not as sovereign, but as destitute and suffering. Indeed, the possibility of a finite community of relation rooted in the recognition of interdependence and nourished by compassion, emerges not in that horrifying moment when Oedipus realizes the inescapable truth and blinds himself with the broaches of his dead wife and mother,[5] but in that moment of transformation at the very end of *Oedipus Tyrannus* when Oedipus, blinded and shattered, reaches out for his daughters. To turn, as Sophocles invites us, from that overwhelming scene of abjection to the tender moment when Oedipus is granted the opportunity to touch his daughters is already to trace the signature of a poetic politics, one we here might further delineate as the politics of the between.[6]

This itinerary pursues three moments of touching, each of which articulates something of the logic of the politics of the between and the ecology endemic to the community it opens.[7]

---

5 Sophocles, *Sophoclis Fabulae, OT,* 1181.
6 For an articulation of the politics of the between as it opens in the work of Hesiod and Aeschylus, see Christopher P. Long, "The Daughters of Metis: Patriarchal Dominion and the Politics of the Between," *The Graduate Faculty Philosophy Journal* 28, no. 2 (2007): 67–86.
7 The term "ecology" here points already in the direction we are heading. Donna Haraway, drawing on the work of M. Beth Dempster, has suggested that human politics is always situated in a complex ecological context that extends beyond the merely human to deeper connections with a wide diversity of creatures with whom we must make kin. See Donna J. Haraway, *Staying with the Trouble: Making Kin in the Chthulucene* (Durham: Duke University Press Books, 2016), 103. This kinship in the making is identified

The first, as has been mentioned, occurs when Oedipus reaches for his daughters at the end of *Oedipus Tyrannus*. It marks the institution of a community between Oedipus and his daughters no longer dominated by patriarchal sovereignty. The second moment of touching occurs in *Oedipus at Colonus* when Ismene and Antigone embrace Oedipus after their abduction by Creon. In this scene, a constellation emerges that beautifully embodies the very structure of the politics of the between. Situated here between Antigone and Ismene, Oedipus is bound to a community of reciprocal support born of a trauma that anticipates the resurgence of the politics of violence and retribution that will condition its ultimate demise. The destitution of this community of compassion between them is marked, however, by a third moment of touching, one that mirrors the first, as Oedipus hands his daughters over to Theseus in a symbolic gesture of nuptial union. The moment is ambiguous and complex — a glimpse of something possible — the nuptial — that all to easily falls back into a patriarchal economy of authority and domination.

The Institution of a Community of Com-passion

Oedipus Tyrannus ends with the death of a patriarch that marks the beginning of a new community rooted in compassion.[8] The

---

as a kind of sympoiesis, which Dempster suggests as a name for "collectively-producing systems that do not have self-defined spatial or temporal boundaries. Information and control are distributed among components." See M. Beth Dempster, "A Self-Organizing Systems Perspective on Planning for Sustainability" (Masters, University of Waterloo, 1998), v, http://www.bethd.ca/pubs/mesthe.pdf. Following Dempster, Haraway further delineates sympoiesis as "a word proper to complex, dynamic, responsive, situated, historical systems. It is a word for worlding-with, in company. Sympoiesis enfolds autopoiesis and generatively unfurls and extends it." See Haraway, *Staying with the Trouble*, 58. Perhaps what we have been tracking as poetic has been sympoietic all along.

8   Gellie traces the stages of development by which "Oedipus finds his way back into the world." See G. Gellie, "The Last Scene of the Oedipus Tyrannus," *Ramus* 15 (1986): 35–42. In his essay on "The End of Sophocles' O.T.," Davies affirms Livingstone's suggestion that Sophocles "realized that with Oedipus blinded and Jocasta dead there remained a dramatic problem and

moment of its incipience can be traced to an imaginative and sympathetic response to a simple human request. Oedipus, now blind and destitute, implores Creon to send his daughters to him: "Most of all, with my hands / let me touch them and bewail these bad things."[9] But Creon seems already to have anticipated this request, for without his ordering it, the children are made present to Oedipus by the sound of their weeping.[10] Oedipus, surprised, asks: "Having compassion for me, has Creon / sent me these most loved, my two offspring?"[11] With this question, Oedipus at once identifies what motivates Creon — compassion (*epoiktiras*) — and affirms the primacy of the love that inspires it.

The community established here is animated by Creon's compassion for Oedipus which has itself grown from his own experiences with Oedipus and his daughters. In affirming his responsibility for the appearance of the girls, Creon articulates what motivated him: "I am he who presented these two girls/for I have come to know the delight [*terpsin*] their presence has so long held for you."[12] This gesture of kindness, rooted as it is in Creon's ethical imagination, is the condition for the possibility of Oedipus's ultimate return to the world of human community. Anticipating his suffering, Creon has brought the best gift he could

---

opportunity. His solution of it produced something as great and imaginative as anything in the play." See M. Davies, "The End of Sophocles' O.T.," *Hermes* 110, no. 3 (1982): 268–78. For the Livingstone text, see Cyril Bailey et al., eds., *Greek Poetry and Life: Essays Presented to Gilbert Murray on His Seventieth Birthday, January 2, 1936* (Oxford: The Clarendon Press, 1936), 158.

9   Sophocles, *Sophoclis Fabulae*, *OT*, 1466–67.
10 Blondell notes that the precise moment of their entrance is a matter of some debate. See Sophocles, *The Theban Plays*, trans. Ruby Blondell (Newburyport: Focus Publishing, 2004), 150n150. Jebb suggests that the children enter at line 1470, which makes dramatic sense. See Richard Claverhouse Jebb, The Oedipus Tyrannus of Sophocles (Cambridge: Cambridge University Press, 1963). Dawe argues that it is 1422. Gellie shows how Sophocles turns our attention to the children in stages, a turning that culminates in their appearance at 1471. See Gellie, "The Last Scene of the Oedipus Tyrannus," 42 n. 14.
11 Sophocles, *Sophoclis Fabulae*, *OT*, 1473–75.
12 Ibid., *OT*, 1476–77.

imagine based on what he has come to know about Oedipus and his daughters. Oedipus had himself already evoked the intimate tenderness that characterizes his relationship with Antigone and Ismene when he asked Creon to attend to his daughters:

> but these two, my miserable, piteous girls
> whose food was never set upon a table apart
> so they never were without this man, but however many things I
> would touch, these two would always have a share of all.[13]

The image is striking not simply because it would have been unusual for a man in classical Athens to dine with his daughters,[14] but also because it articulates an intimacy of relation rooted in the common practices of everyday nourishment and generosity. This intimacy is amplified by the emphasis Oedipus places on physical proximity and the centrality of touch.

Yet the logic of touch here, however tender, remains caught within a paternalistic economy of dependence. The father welcomes his daughters to the table "so they never were without this man;" he shares *his* food with them, but there is no indication that he received nourishment in return. Thus, the deep political significance of Creon's imaginative gift to Oedipus in his most acute time of need lies in the recognition that the delight Oedipus had always taken in the presence of his daughters was a sign of a latent reciprocity capable of opening them to a more symbiotic mode of relation. The phenomenon of touch literally embodies the reciprocity endemic to the relationship that now opens between them. This fundamental shift and, indeed, the moment a new possibility for political community is born, can be heard in the words Oedipus speaks as he finally embraces the girls:

---

13 Ibid., *OT*, 1462–65.
14 See Sophocles, *The Theban Plays*, 150n149. Blondell notes that this passage suggests that the heroic age may not have shared the strict norms governing the father/child relationship that operated in the classical period.

> Come
> to these brother's hands of mine
> which made the once shining eyes
> of the father who begot you both, see thus,
> the father, seeing nothing, questioning nothing
> now revealed having sown you, children, in the place he was sown.
> I weep also for you...[15]

The delight of the father, rooted as it too often is in a detached and objectifying gaze, has here transformed itself into a brother's touch and settled thus symbolically into a more equal and reciprocal ecological community.[16] As sovereign, the father sees without himself being seen and his touch nourishes mere dependence; as brother, the touch of the father is recognized as reciprocal, for to touch is always also to be touched in return.[17] Seeing his own limits, Oedipus is nourished by this interdependence. Although he remains father, he now also enters into relation with his daughters as a brother and, in so doing, he sets aside the detached, unreflective, and oppressive gaze of sovereignty. The possibility of a politics other than that of patriarchal domination emerges here, the moment Oedipus is empowered,

---

15 Sophocles, *Sophoclis Fabulae*, 1481–86.
16 In Callimachus's *Hymn to Artemis*, a nine-year old Artemis delights her father as she vainly tries to stretch her little hands up to touch his beard, a gesture that causes him to grant her all she desires. See Callimachus, *CalThe Hymns*, ed. and trans. Susan A. Stephens (Oxford: Oxford University Press, 2015). The image reinforces a logic of relation in which the daughter appears delightful in her attempts to touch her father and so solicits his caress and indulgence. There is reciprocity here, but no equality. For a discussion of this scene, see Karl Kerínyi, "A Mythological Image of Girlhood," in *Facing the Gods*, ed. James Hillman (Irving: Spring Publications, 1980), 39–45.
17 See Maurice Merleau-Ponty, *Phenomenology of Perception*, trans. Colin Smith, 2nd edn. (London and New York: Routledge, 2002), 106–7. In chapter 4 of the *The Visible and the Invisible*, Merleau-Ponty writes: "There is a circle of the touched and the touching, the touch takes hold of the touching…." See Maurice Merleau-Ponty, *The Visible and the Invisible*, ed. Claude Lefort, trans. Alphonso Lingis, 1st edn. (Northwestern University Press, 1968), 143.

by virtue of Creon's imaginative gift and the painful recognition of his own finitude, to embrace his daughters in a sympoietic community of com-passion, of co-suffering. His recognition of their suffering as his own and of his suffering as theirs is at the root of the community of com-passion that is born here and flourishes for a time at Colonus.

Although Oedipus's return to the palace of Thebes at the end of *Oedipus Tyrannus* suggests indeed that he has been returned to the world of human community, that institution of patriarchal authority proved ultimately unable to contain a figure of such abjection. If, in Julia Kristeva's language, the abject names "the jettisoned object" that "is radically excluded" and draws one "toward the place where meaning collapses," then the final scene of *Oedipus Tyrannus* can be heard to announce the death of a sovereign and the beginning of a life of abjection that leads Oedipus, Antigone, and Ismene to the grove of the Eumenides at Colonus on the outskirts of Athens. Here, however, the logic of another politics can be discerned. Kristiva points to it when she writes: "the abjection of Oedipus at Colonus is the *not knowing* of the speaking being who is *subject to death* at the same time as to *symbolic union*."[18] The violent attack on his own eyes, those vehicles of sight and symbols of knowing, mark Oedipus's recognition of his own subjection to death; and yet the moment he relinquishes his hubris and reconciles himself to his own finitude — "let my fate take me where it will"[19] — he reaches out for his daughters. In utter abjection, Oedipus turns to his daughters; and when they ultimately embrace they lament together and take solace in the simple comfort of the common touch of their being-together. The union to which Oedipus is returned, then, is not governed by the symbolic economy of patriarchal authority, but rooted rather in the vernacular of touch and nourished by the reciprocal intimacy endemic to the deep recognition of finitude and interdependence. The union enacted

---

18 Julia Kristeva, *Powers of Horror: An Essay on Abjection*, trans. Leon S. Roudiez (New York: Columbia University Press, 1982), 87.
19 Sophocles, *Sophoclis Fabulae*, OT, 1458.

here between them is nuptial, insistently contingent, ineluctably situated between natality and mortality, attuned and responsive to what comes to presence there.[20]

Between Antigone and Ismene at Colonus

This touching scene at the end of *Oedipus Tyrannus* anticipates a second moment of embracing now from *Oedipus at Colonus* when Theseus returns Ismene and Antigone to Oedipus after they have been abducted by Creon. If the first scene is made possible by Creon's imaginative gift, rooted as it is in the recognition of the longstanding delight Oedipus had always taken in his daughters, the second manifests this delight now transformed into a reciprocal relation of interdependence. Here is how the scene unfolds:

> OEDIPUS: Come to your father, children; give your bodies for me to embrace, having been made present beyond all hope.
> ANTIGONE: You shall have what you want, for this favor we yearn together.
> OEDIPUS: Where, indeed, where are you?
> ANTIGONE: We are here together close to you.
> [Oedipus and his daughters embrace.]
> OEDIPUS: Most beloved offspring! ANTIGONE: For this parent, all love.
> OEDIPUS: Oh supports of light [*ō skēptra photos*]. ANTIGONE: Ill-fated daughters of an ill-fated father.
> OEDIPUS: I have the things I love most, death would no longer make me all-wretched, with you two placed beside me. Press close upon my ribs, children, on both sides

---

[20] Here something like the nomadic subjectivity of which Rosi Braidotti speaks shows itself. Exiled from Thebes, Oedipus becomes a nomad, fully reliant on his relationship with his daughters. Braidotti writes that nomadic subjectivity "combines non-unitary subjectivity with ethical accountability by foregrounding the ontological role played by relationality." See Rosi Braidotti, *The Posthuman* (Cambridge and Malden: Polity Press, 2013), 93.

growing together with him from whom you grew, and rest,
once desolate, from that unhappy wandering.
And tell me the things that happened as briefly as possible, since
little speech suffices for girls your age.[21]

This poignant scene of reciprocal support and love is expressed again in the vernacular of touch in which the girls are said to be "supports of light" that press upon the ribs of Oedipus from both sides. And if Oedipus returns in that final sentence to an ancient paternalism in which the women are discouraged from speaking at length, this touching scene points symbolically to an ecology of relation other than that of patriarchal dominion.[22] Theseus himself recognizes this picture of Oedipus situated between his daughters, holding them and being held by them, as rooted "in your delight [*tertheis*] with these two children."[23] This delight, unlike that with which Creon had grown familiar, is not conditioned primarily by paternal superiority and juvenile dependence. Rather, it suggests a nuptial relation that has grown over the course of their unhappy wanderings during which time Oedipus has learned to lean upon Antigone and Ismene, and they, in turn, have found their voice.

To discern the contours of this nuptial relation rooted in mutual dependence and shared suffering, it will be necessary to trace in the symbolic power of the image of Oedipus situated between his daughters the possibility of another politics, one in which the father becomes a brother, and these sisters,

---

21 Sophocles, *Sophoclis Fabulae*, OC, 1104–16.
22 In his funeral oration, Pericles gives voice to the ancient paternalism mentioned here in his infamous injunction that women should give little occasion for rumor. See Thucydides, *Historiae I* (Oxford: Oxford University Press, 1942), ii 45.2. For a brief discussion of this, see, Christopher P. Long, "Dancing Naked with Socrates: Pericles, Aspasia and Socrates at Play with Politics, Rhetoric and Philosophy," *Ancient Philosophy* 23, no. 1 (2003): 49–69, at 64. For more detail, see William Blake Tyrrell and Larry J. Bennett, "Pericles' Muting of Women's Voices in Thuc. 2.45.2," *The Classical Journal* 95, no. 1 (1999): 37–51.
23 Sophocles, *Sophoclis Fabulae*, OC, 1140.

each in her own way, come to embody those excellences capable of cultivating a community of compassion. The political efficacy of the community that has grown between Oedipus and his daughters can be felt in the impact it had on Theseus and the city of Athens, for their willingness to host these abject subjects is symbolically rewarded in the end as the nuptial union between Oedipus and his daughters is handed down to Theseus and the prophesy that secures the welfare of the city in which Oedipus is buried is fulfilled.

The symbolic importance of the grove of the Eumenides as the site in which the nuptial community is nurtured can only be fully appreciated if it is allowed to resonate against the story of Agamemnon and Iphigeneia.[24] At the end of Aeschylus's *Oresteia*, Athena forgives Orestes for killing his mother, Clytemnestra, in retribution for her murder of his father, Agamemnon. Athena acquits Orestes because it seems to be the will of Zeus and, as she says, "I am with my heart very much on the side of my father."[25] Recognizing that this decision will further exacerbate the anger of the Furies, those old goddesses of vengeance who had been pursuing Orestes for the murder of Clytemnestra, Athena succeeds in persuading them to give up their claims to justice in terms of violence and retribution by offering them a place of honor in the city.[26] It is precisely this place of honor and the recognition that comes with it that marks the transformation of a politics of vengeance driven by the logic of force into a politics of compassion rooted in the power of persuasion. This, indeed, is the site to which Antigone leads her father at the beginning of *Oedipus at Colonus* and it is the site to

---

24 See R.P. Winnington-Ingram, "A Religious Function of Greek Tragedy: A Study in the Oedipus Coloneus and the Oresteia," *The Journal of Hellenic Studies* 74 (1954): 16–24. Winnington-Ingram recognizes the tight connection between the *Oresteia* and *Oedipus at Colonus*, suggesting that to some degree in *Oedipus at Colonus* Sophocles grapples with the hope with which the *Oresteia* ends.
25 Alan H. Sommerstein, *Aeschylus Eumenides* (Cambridge: Cambridge University Press, 1989), l. 738.
26 For a detailed discussion of the complex and politically salient manner in which Athena persuades the Furies, see Long, "The Daughters of Metis."

which Ismene courageously returns in the hope of performing a rite in honor of the goddesses when she is taken by the force of the hands of Creon.[27]

Thus, in articulating the excellences these two daughters of Oedipus embody, it will also be necessary to attend to the site where these excellences are performed; for the grove of the Eumenides marks the struggle between the politics of patriarchal domination driven by the compulsion to grasp and possess and the politics of nuptial compassion animated by reciprocity and recognition.[28] In and around the sacred grove of the Eumenides, a politics rooted not in violence and retribution, but in mutual dependence, compassion, and respect emerges for a moment before succumbing again to the repetition compulsion endemic to the logic of patriarchal dominion.

Antigone and Ismene: Sources of Another Power

The *Oedipus at Colonus* opens with the tender picture of a father dependent upon his daughter and of a daughter who has herself come to embody the attentive responsiveness that makes her an excellent leader. Oedipus has come to depend upon Antigone and, even if he does not yet recognize it as a blessing, he has acclimated to this dependence.[29] He asks her where they

---

27 Sophocles, *Sophoclis Fabulae, OC*, 818–19 and 830. There Creon says: "I will not touch this man, but only her who's mine." The touch of Creon here has the violence of the grasp and the intent to possess. It is the touch of the patriarch.

28 See Darice Birge, "The Grove of the Eumenides: Refuge and Hero Shrine in *Oedipus at Colonus*," *The Classical Journal* 80, no. 1 (1984): 11–17. Birge does not thematize the grove in political terms, emphasizing instead the relation between the human and the divine it seems to signify. However, given the parallel between Athena's success persuading the Eumenides and Antigone's ultimate failure to persuade Oedipus and Polyneices and given the manner in which Polyneices identifies Oedipus with the Furies at the end, the site of the grove may be heard to host a transformation in the opposite direction of the one Aeschylus articulates in the Oresteia.

29 Oedipus tells the chorus who asks who he is: "One not entirely to be called blessed for the first of destinies, you who are the guardians over this land. But that's clear. Otherwise I would not move thus with another's eyes, or

are and she is his eyes.[30] When he needs to sit, she anticipates, and guarding him, says "the need for this is something I have learned from time."[31] Living in intimate connection together, exiled and alone, pariahs, the relationship between them has cultivated certain embodied habits of being-together that find their expression here in their interaction with the chorus at the sacred grove of the Eumenides.

These embodied habits articulate a set of excellences that belong to the nuptial. Here the integrated corporeal relationship between Antigone and Oedipus point symbolically to the possibilities that open when a father relinquishes his obsession with sovereignty and embraces an interdependent relation with his daughter.[32] Symbolically, where father becomes brother, the patriarchal authority breaks down and a new possibility for being-together emerges.

Upon seeing them seated in the sacred grove, the chorus of noble men from Colonus demands they depart. Oedipus seeks the advice of his daughter and she wisely counsels him to listen: "Father, it is necessary to care equally for the townspeople, yielding and listening to the things required."[33] Reaching out, she touches him as she leads him away and, now for a second time in the first scene of the drama, helps him to sit. The way

---

be anchored, great as I am, on the small." See Sophocles, *Sophoclis Fabulae*, OC, 144–49. Oedipus, it seems, remains bound to a logic of grandeur that does not fit his position, but might ultimately be earned by the way he comports himself in it. That, however, remains an open question given the way he responds to his sons.

30 Ibid., OC, 1–20. See also 138: "I see by voice…" and 866, where Oedipus calls Antigone his "unarmed eye".

31 Ibid., OC, 22.

32 Maurice Hamington, drawing on the work of Nel Noddings, identifies the mutual relationship thematized here as "integrated at the corporeal level" and as a kind of "super-attentiveness." See Maurice Hamington, "A Father's Touch: Caring Embodiment and a Moral Revolution," in *Revealing Male Bodies* (Bloomington: Indiana University Press, 2002), 274. That essay beautifully articulates the importance of the father's touch for the ethical education of daughters.

33 Sophocles, *Sophoclis Fabulae*, OC, 171–72.

she settles him into place beautifully articulates the embodied reciprocity of their relationship:

> ANTIGONE: Father, this task is mine; in peace
> fit step with step...
> OEDIPUS: Oh, alas, alas!
> ANTIGONE: ... leaning your aged body
> into my loving arms.[34]

We are made here to feel something of the intimate connection that has grown between these two over time as she gently takes him into her arms, reversing the directionality of the relationship established in that first moment of embrace at the end of Oedipus's life as king. Receiving something of his suffering as her own, she empowers him to sit. Thus, indeed, she has become his support, the source of his power — she has become his scepter. The Greek *skēptron* means both walking stick and scepter — the symbol of regal authority. Oedipus, indeed, assaulted his own father with just such a *skēptron,* thereby unknowingly winning for himself the authority that was his own demise.[35] Now, however, Oedipus's power lies with his daughters, for they have become the scepters that Creon will explicitly seek to take from him.[36]

The ambiguity of the *skēptron* points to the underlying *political* significance of Oedipus's relationship with his daughters. With Antigone, the power of their nuptial union and the source of their ability to establish connections with others lies in her attentive responsiveness to his embodied suffering and her attuned ability to respond to the situation in which they find themselves. He looks to her for advice; in giving it, she lends him courage to go on. With Ismene, on the other hand, the nuptial relation between them is shown to be conditioned by the excellences of

---

34 Ibid., *OC,* 198–201.
35 Ibid., *OT,* 810–11. For a discussion of the significance of the double meaning of the *skēptron* and the changing significance it takes in the *Oedipus at Colonus,* see Sophocles, *The Theban Plays,* 12.
36 Sophocles, *Sophoclis Fabulae, OC,* 848–50.

resourceful independence and the tenacious courage to speak in one's own voice. These are the excellences that show themselves in the striking scene of her first appearance.

Catching sight of her, Antigone exclaims in shock. When Oedipus asks confusedly what is happening, Antigone resorts to description in a caring attempt to offer insight to her father: she sees a woman approaching on horseback with a wide-brimmed hat to protect her from the sun. Bright glances from her eyes meet Antigone confirming the presence of Ismene, her sister. This is a compelling image of feminine independence and sisterly connection. Arriving in the direction from Thebes, Ismene emphasizes how difficult it was to find them and how difficult it is now to see them through her tears of pain.[37] The scene continues to unfold this way:

> OEDIPUS: Touch me, daughter. ISMENE: I am touching you both.
> OEDIPUS: Seed of the same blood. ISMENE: Oh miserable nurture.
> OEDIPUS: Of her and me? ISMENE: And my miserable self as third.
> OEDIPUS: Why did you come, child? ISMENE: From concern [*promēthia*] for you.
> OEDIPUS: Was it from a longing desire [*pothoisi*]? Ismene: And to bring you these words myself
> together with the only house-slave I could trust.[38]

Established by touch, this community of three is conditioned by caring forethought [*promēthia*], a yearning for connection and, indeed, a need to speak in one's own voice news that will be difficult to bear. Ismene appears as a figure of independent courage willing to risk her life for those she loves.

---

37 Ibid., *OC*, 310–26.
38 Ibid., *OC*, 329–34.

The Resurgence of Patriarchal Violence

Ismene reports the struggle for sovereignty between her brothers and so announces the resurgence of the masculine grasp for patriarchal dominion that will ultimately destroy the possibility of community these three symbolically embody. Oedipus himself puts the point succinctly in response to Ismene when she relates that the boys well know the Delphic pronouncement that whosoever possesses the body of Oedipus will be protected. Repeating his use of the Greek *pothos* — longing desire — Oedipus expresses disdainful anger, asking "do those evil ones, hearing this, / place kingly authority above their longing desire for myself?"[39] Enraged, Oedipus utters for the first of two times the curse upon his sons that will bring the destitution of his two beloved daughters: "May the gods then never extinguish their predestined strife...then neither will the one who now has the scepter / and throne remain, nor will the other who's gone / ever return."[40] The long tutelage in cultivating the habits of compassion here shows itself incapable of suppressing the resurgence of rage that initiates the repetition of violence which sets the community once again along a tragic path.

Yet the voice of Antigone stands against this compulsion to repeat the violence endemic to the logic of patriarchal dominion. Perhaps drawing strength from the courage of her sister, and perhaps too from the sacred grove of those goddesses who stand for the transformative efficacy of political persuasion, Antigone valiantly seeks first to turn her father from his rage and then her brother from self-destruction.

When Oedipus refuses even to grant Polyneices a hearing, Antigone attempts to persuade her father not to impiously trade evil for evil. She counsels him to respect Polyneices and to re-

---

39 Ibid., *OC*, 418–19.
40 Ibid., *OC*, 421–27. Oedipus continues with the juxtaposition of his sons and daughters, insisting that while his sons drove him from the land by force and chose the scepter, throne and kinship over their father, his daughters gave him nurturance of life, security and the aid of kinship. See ibid., *OC*, 440–50. Cf. 1365–68.

flect upon the present situation from an intergenerational perspective so these actions may be understood within the context of the wider history of troubles related to his own relationship to his parents. Oedipus allows himself to be convinced at least to give a hearing to his son. Words, it seems, have the power to bring him this far; but his old anger dies hard, and he is unable to rise above it, despite the wisdom of a daughter's voice.[41]

The voice of a sister too proves incapable of moving the brother from the path of self-destruction. Upon the rearticulation of their father's curse upon his sons, a curse indeed, that appeals explicitly to the ancient law of Justice which Polyneices himself rightly identifies with the Furies, Antigone seeks to use the persuasive power of words to intervene with him as Athena did with them.[42] She enjoins him to turn his army back, wondering what use it is to rage against one's fatherland. And she articulates well how Polyneices' response, caught up as it is in that destructive masculine logic of shame and honor, will itself bring about what Oedipus prophesied.[43] The path of her own destruction is here set, for in a twisted reversal of values, Antigone's own attentive concern for her brother, her willingness to be persuaded by him not to allow his body to be dishonored, is precisely what will bring about her own destitution in the final frame of the story, the tragedy that bears her name.

And yet, *this* drama, *Oedipus at Colonus,* does not end with the double failure of Antigone's words. Rather, it builds again toward a more hopeful possibility, for if Antigone's voice falls

---

41 Ibid., *OC,* 1181ff. Antigone seems to recognize the power of words to move people when she encourages Polyneices to continue to talk despite Oedipus's silence: "Abundant words, which give delight / or show distress or stir up pity in some way, / sometimes impart a voice to those whose voice was mute" (1281–83, Blondell trans.)

42 Oedipus appeals to the ancient law of Justice at 1382 and Polyneices identifies his father with the Furies at 1434.

43 Sophocles, *Sophoclis Fabulae, OC,* 1414–46. The masculine logic of anger, shame and honor shows itself to be self-destructive three times over in the trilogy — Oedipus and Liaus: they would have killed me (546–48 — still the impoverished *pros dikas ti* but this certain justice is impoverished), the violence of Polyneices, and then that of Creon in the Antigone.

upon the deaf ears of Oedipus and Polyneices, it is perhaps heard by Theseus, for he too was there when she offered counsel to her father and he shows himself compassionate and open to persuasion. Thus, it is perhaps decisive that Sophocles ends this story and Oedipus's mortal life with a marriage ritual of sorts — a gesture toward the nuptial — whereby the touch of the father is bequeathed to Theseus, the King of Athena's city. Upon hearing the thunder that calls him to his grave, Oedipus touches his daughters one final time. Folding them in his arms, he announces his own death and seeks to comfort them, saying aloud what was said by touch before: "you have never been loved by anyone more / than this man here, of whom you will be deprived / for the remainder of this life."[44] The messenger reports that they remained there, weeping together, holding one another; and when these lamentations of compassion grew silent, a voice called Oedipus to his death. Before he goes, however, he asks Theseus: "Dear friend, give to my girls / the ancient trust of your right hand, and daughters, yours to him," as if this nuptial gesture of touching reciprocity might nurture once again a community of compassion capable of undermining the compulsive repetition of patriarchal violence.

Here for a moment, the possibility of another politics shows itself, one determined neither by the compulsion to dominate nor by the self-defeating cycle of retribution. Rather, the reciprocity of this final touch points to a politics, difficult, but possible, animated by a longing for connection rooted in a deep recognition of finite interdependence. Symbolically in the tragic poetry of Sophocles, this other politics grows between Oedipus and his daughters and lives for a moment at Colonus, nourished by the excellences they embody, before it is handed down as a legacy to Theseus so that his city, Athena's city, might flourish.

---

44 Ibid., *OC*, 1617–19.

The Cultivated the Habits of Nuptial Response-ability

The poetic politics to which the Sophoclean text gestures symbolically continues to be eclipsed by the calcified and self-destructive habits of a patriarchal politics that teaches us again and again the deepest lessons of tragic denial. Yet, again and again, we fail to learn through suffering (*pathei mathos*), compulsively positing principles that perpetuate a violence and injustice rooted ultimately in our unwillingness to come to terms with our own finitude. If, however, the symbols to which Sophocles gestures give us something to do, perhaps we might return now again for a final time, to the beginning, which, as Schürmann always reminded us, ought to be sought in what is most familiar, however poorly understood.

The owl of Minerva, as Hegel has suggested, spreads its wings at dusk.[45] So too now at the end of the day, we will do well to return to the question with which Schürmann concludes *Broken Hegemonies*, a question that has haunted this text from the beginning as we have sought to listen to Aristotle, Plotinus, and Kant, for habits and practices that might begin to embody a response. Recall the question again here now: "With eyes opened by the hubristic sufferings that our age has inflicted on itself — as Oedipus at Colonus wants his eyes open and who thought of his eyes as open — is it possible to love ultimates in differend?"[46] Recall too, however, that what appears at the end of *Broken Hegemonies* as a question, was posited on that fall September day in 1991 as a genuine possibility; for there Schürmann had said, and later published, "it is possible to love differing ultimates. This, I submit, would be expanding the limits of imagination."[47]

---

45 Georg Wilhelm Friedrich Hegel, Georg Lasson, and Eduard Gans, *Grundlinien der Philosophie des Rechts* (Leipzig: F. Meiner, 1911), 17. A more literal translation would be: "The Owl of Minerva first begins its flight with the spreading of the dusk."

46 Schürmann, *Broken Hegemonies*, 631.

47 Reiner Schürmann, "Conditions of Evil," in *Deconstruction and the Possibility of Justice*, eds. Drucilla Cornell, Michel Rosenfeld, and David Gray Carlson (New York: Routledge, 1992), 400.

This invitation to expand the limits of imagination in order to discern a politics rooted in the capacity to love ultimates in differend set us on the path we have now traversed. If, as Hannah Arendt has suggested, "to think with an enlarged mentality means that one trains one's imagination to go visiting,"[48] perhaps we might return here at the end to the sites our imagination has visited over the course of our journey in an attempt to think with an enlarged mentality and indeed put into practice, through an imagination now expanded, the habits of nuptial response-ability that empower us to love ultimates in differend so that we might create more just and enriching lives together.

Our journey remained attuned always to the rhythms of the day signaled in the riddle of the Sphinx and brought to life in the poetry of Char. In the "morning heaviness," Aristotle wakened us to the habits of beginning; to "crown the noon," Plotinus gestured to the habits of living; and in the evening, the "supposed end" that marks also a "new innocence," Kant reminded us of the habits of dying. These three, woven together, enable us to settle into the ravaged site of rapture, conditioned at once by mortal natality and natal mortality, at home in a network of potentials and alive to the possibilities of justice that linger here.

In the morning, Aristotle uncovers the topography of the site we must learn to inhabit together. It is a place of encounter in which what appears refuses also to give itself over fully so that each attempt to create community is held accountable to what remains inaccessible. Here already at the beginning, we are made to recognize the limits that condition our attempts to live together. In Aristotle, those limits come to language in the little words *tode ti* that point already to the duplicity of beginning, holding each attempt to posit an unequivocal principle of authority accountable to that which escapes every thetic gesture of archic dominion. Here we began to discern a poetics capable of responding to what appears in ways that do justice to duplicity and open new possibilities for community. This ability to

---

48 Hannah Arendt, *Lectures on Kant's Political Philosophy* (Chicago: University of Chicago Press, 1982), 43.

respond is rooted in a certain compassion, a suffering together attuned to the limits that condition our life together. Aristotle wakens us to the complexity of things, to the rich plurality of the earth on which we dwell and the network of potentials we encounter here. To flourish in this place requires the cultivation of an ethical imagination capable of ecological justice, an imagination, indeed, expansive enough to open us to new, more just ways of living together.[49] What comes to language, however, in the *tode ti* with respect to the encountered individual must here now be heard to extend beyond the dichotomy between subject and object to a deeper complexity at work in every attempted gathering, for that to which singularity had referred in our reading of Aristotle must now be recognized as endemic to a whole ecology of relationships at play whenever a plurality of beings attempt to put justice into practice in community with one another. The ravage site of rapture turns out to be ravaged by a fecund plurality at its surface and in its depth, from differences between individuals, perceived and unrecognized, to differences between beings, animate and inanimate, from diversities of experiences to divergent histories. The intersectional differences that ravage this site are also the source of its rapture, the play of powers and possibilities that attune us to one another and empower us to imagine together, to sympoetically practice, a politics that enables flourishing without recourse to an ultimate principle of dominion that denies the discordant play of natality and mortality.

The distance we have travelled can now be heard in the shift in our vocabulary from of poetics to sympoetics and from differend to discordance. We have traced the signature of these shifts along the way, but here justice requires us to make it as explicit as possible. Schürmann himself demonstrates the way forward when he delineates the distinction between differend and

---

49 In returning here at the end to ethical imagination and ecological justice, there is an attempt to deepen and refine the ethics of truth articulated at the end of Christopher P. Long, *Aristotle on the Nature of Truth* (New York: Cambridge University Press, 2011), 251–53.

discord. The differend remains situated within the hegemonic logic of competing laws and thus fails to recognize the pull of mortality that conditions its legislative practices. Discordance, however, describes a political site ravaged by the conditions of natality and mortality that somehow sustains it. The term itself holds the disintegrative dimension of mortality (dis-) together with the life-giving power of natality (-cord, from the Latin for "heart"), and so gives voice to the incongruous manner in which life joins with death without consolidating under a common authority. To inhabit such a political site riven by discord without becoming, quite literally, disheartened, requires us to undertake a kind of making together, *sumpoēisis,* rooted in the shared suffering of tragic knowledge. The poetics of politics here give way to a sympoetic engagement that enjoins us to cultivate habits of thinking and acting that enable us to settle into the discordant site of nuptial gathering.

If in the morning heaviness we are made to feel the weight of the duplicity of beginning even as we are asked to resist the compulsion to posit yet another ultimate principle that would institute yet another broken hegemony, as the sun mounts to crown the noon, we find in the thinking of Plotinus, practices of the self that might enable us to settle into the discordant site of nuptial union. We encountered these practices in the very middle of the middle panel of our tryptic, where Plotinus sought to bring his experience of union with the one to language. There we heard the language itself falter, an echo of Agamemnon's trembling voice, and yet with a more hopeful inflection; for Plotinus seeks to give voice not to a horror that cannot be spoken, but to a rapturous beauty beyond the limits of thinking and imagination. In so doing, Plotinus articulates a way of being united rooted in certain practices of the self. And even if the shift from a poetics to a sympoietics of politics requires us to relinquish the hegemony of the self, as Kant's own trembling voice intimated, still, as a site of nuptial response-ability, the self retains enough coherence to enable us to hold one another accountable as we attempt to create together political communities animated by a concern for ecological justice.

As we've heard, in his attempts to give voice to the event of union with the one, Plotinus indicates that this way of being united unfolds not through pure contemplation, but through an expansive imagination or, as Plotinus puts it, through:

> [A]nother kind of seeing, a being out of oneself [*exstasis*] and simplifying [*haplōsis*] and giving oneself over [*epidosis*] and pressing toward contact [*ephesis pros haphēn*] and coming to rest [*stasis*] and sustaining thought that leads to union [*perinoēsis pros epharmogēn*].[50]

The text is eloquent, held together by a chain of conjunctions that lead us to a kind of union that comes through sustained thought to language as *epharmogēn,* a word that names a kind of adaptation, a coincidence made possible by adjustment and an abiding capacity for accommodation.[51] In his reading of the text, Schürmann had rightly emphasized that this way of being united opens us to another natality, to what he there called "pure natality," in order to distinguish it from the natality associated with hegemonic maximization.[52] We have traced the contours of this pure natality to the event of union — the nuptial. Here, however, we are able to discern certain practices of the self that open us to the nuptial and to the abilities of response that make such communion possible. Perhaps we can linger a moment here on each one, even as the sun that crowned the noon begins to edge toward dusk.

Nuptial union requires us, first, to stand outside of ourselves. But the ecstasy to which Plotinus gestures here is quite the opposite of the loss of self commonly associated with ecstatic mysticism. Rather, the attempt to stand out of oneself is said to require us to simplify, give ourselves over to the other, press toward contact and come to settled rest. The course charted here

---

50 *En*. VI.9 [9], 11, 23–25.
51 See George Henry Liddell and Robert Scott, *A Greek–English Lexicon* (Oxford: The Clarendon Press, 1968), s.v. *epharmogē*.
52 Schürmann, *Broken Hegemonies,* 156.

is precisely the path Sophocles shows Oedipus himself following in the wake of the cathartic encounter with his own finitude that blinded him. The contours of the community of com-passion we traced in our reading of *Oedipus at Colonus* are here in Plotinus amplified. Blinded, Oedipus opens himself to another seeing that enables him to stand outside of himself in a different way, no longer as sovereign, but now as a caring father more deeply attuned to the limits endemic to his finite nature. This attunement to finitude is an important dimension of what Plotinus calls simplification, for it involves a pealing back from the surface of things to uncover the ontological conditions of finite existence. Simplification empowers us to encounter that with which we are all familiar, though poorly: the ultimate conditions of natality and mortality. However traumatic this simplification was for Oedipus, still it enabled to give himself over to his daughters, to press toward contact with them, and ultimately, in the grove of the Eumenides at Colonus, to come to rest having learned with his daughters somehow to adjust to the world they inhabit. The union they establish at Colonus is nuptial, for it is rooted in a deep recognition of finitude and animated by a "pure natality" uninterested in hegemonic maximization.

The practices of the self to which Plotinus gives voice and Sophocles symbolically enacts point to the habits of nuptial response-ability that might open us to a sympoetic politics oriented toward ecological justice. Stand outside of oneself: enter into relation. Simplify: attend to the irreducible ultimates that condition our relationships, natality and mortality *both*. Give oneself over: relinquish delusions of authority and autonomy. Press toward contact: risk being changed through encounter, embody the courage for chiastic transformation. Come to rest: allow the habits of nuptial response-ability to settle us into the discordant site we inhabit together. Sustain a thinking that enables us to adapt, to accommodate one another, to adjust to the complex network of potentials at play in nuptial union. The thinking sustained here itself stands outside of itself, pressing toward an expanded and expansive imagination, an ethical imagination capable of discerning what justice might be possible here at the discordant site of nuptial community.

Now, as dusk gives way to night, we might finally return to the habits of mortality we encountered in the trembling voice of Kant which announced the crumbling of the subject under the delusion of its own legislative authority. Schürmann had in that context named the condition of mortality that fractures every referent posited as ultimate a *singularization to come*. Inheriting this formulation, we called the condition of natality that holds itself accountable to finitude and open always to new possibilities for community a *philosophy to come*. Here at the close of the day, however, we might now discern through the darkness a *politics to come*, elusive but possible, attuned to the chiastic play of mortality and natality at the discordant site of nuptial gathering. Such a politics to come would need to be sympoetic, co-created in and with a playful and response-able network of potentials audacious enough to resist the tendency to seek solace in absolutes, generous enough to empower ecological flourishing, and gentle enough to do justice to the beautiful complexity of a life acutely attuned to and yet also urgently nourished by its end.

Bibliography

Adorno, Theodor W. *Negative Dialectics*. Translated by E.B. Ashton. New York: Continuum, 1994.
Aeschylus, J.D. Denniston, and Denys Lionel Page. *Agamemnon*. Oxford: Clarendon Press, 1960.
Arendt, Hannah. *Lectures on Kant's Political Philosophy*. Chicago: University of Chicago Press, 1982.
———. *The Human Condition*. Chicago: University of Chicago Press, 1958.
Aristotle. *Aristotelis Analytica Priora et Posteriora*. Oxford: Oxford University Press, 1964.
———. *Aristotelis Ethica Nicomachea*. Oxford: Oxford University Press, 1894.
———. *Aristotelis Metaphysica*. Oxford: Oxford University Press, 1992.
———. *Aristotelis Physica*. Oxford: Oxford University Press, 1992.
Aristotle, and Rudolf Kassel. *Aristotelis De Arte Poetica Liber*. Oxonii: E Typographeo Clarendoniano, 1966.
Armstrong, A.H. "'Emanation' in Plotinus." *Mind* 46 (1937): 61–66. DOI: 10.1093/mind/XLVI.181.61.
Bailey, Cyril, E.A Barber, C.M. Bowra, J.D. Denniston, and D.L. Page, eds. *Greek Poetry and Life: Essays Presented to Gilbert Murray on His Seventieth Birthday, January 2, 1936*. Oxford: The Clarendon Press, 1936.

Beierwaltes, Werner. *Über Ewigkeit und Zeit (Enneade III 7)*. Frankfurt am Main: Vittorio Klosterman, 1995.

Bianchi, Emanuela. "Natal Bodies, Mortal Bodies, Sexual Bodies: Reading Gender, Desire, and Kinship through Reiner Schürmann's *Broken Hegemonies*." *Graduate Faculty Philosophy Journal* 33, no. 1 (April 1, 2012): 57–84. DOI: 10.5840/gfpj20123314.

———. *The Feminine Symptom: Aleatory Matter in the Aristotelian Cosmos*. 1st edn. New York: Fordham University Press, 2014.

Birge, Darice. "The Grove of the Eumenides: Refuge and Hero Shrine in *Oedipus at Colonus*." *The Classical Journal* 80, no. 1 (1984): 11–17. http://www.jstor.org/stable/3297392.

Braidotti, Rosi. *The Posthuman*. Cambridge and Malden: Polity Press, 2013.

Callimachus. *The Hymns*. Edited and translated by Susan A. Stephens. Oxford: Oxford University Press, 2015.

Char, René. *The Dawn Breakers/Les Matinaux*. Newcastle on Tyne: Bloodaxe Books, 1992.

———. *Fureur et mystère*. Paris: Gallimard, 1962.

Davies, M. "The End of Sophocles' O.T." *Hermes* 110, no. 3 (1982): 268–78. http://www.jstor.org/stable/4476265.

Dempster, M. Beth. "A Self-Organizing Systems Perspective on Planning for Sustainability." Masters, University of Waterloo, 1998. http://www.bethd.ca/pubs/mesthe.pdf.

Derrida, Jacques. *Margins of Philosophy*. Translated by Alan Bass. Chicago: University of Chicago Press, 1982.

Ferejohn, Michael. "The Definition of Generated Composites." In *Unity, Identity, and Explanation in Aristotle's Metaphysics,* edited by Theodore Scaltsas, David Charles, and Mary Louise Gill, 291–319. Oxford: Clarendon Press, 1994.

Freud, Sigmund. "Beyond the Pleasure Principle." In *The Standard Edition of the Complete Psychological Works of Sigmund Freud, Vol. 18: Beyond the Pleasure Principle, Group Psychology and Other Works,* translated by James Strachey in collaboration with Anna Freud (London: Hogarth Press, 1955).

———. *The Standard Edition of the Complete Psychological Works of Sigmund Freud, Vol. 19: The Ego and the Id and Other Works*. Translated by James Strachey in collaboration with Anna Freud. London: Hogarth Press, 1955.

Gasché, Rodolphe. "Hegemonic Fantasms." *Research in Phenomenology* 35 (2005): 311–26. DOI: 10.1163/1569164054905375.

Gellie, G. "The Last Scene of the Oedipus Tyrannus." *Ramus* 15 (1986): 35–42. DOI: 10.1017/S0048671X00003428.

Goldman, Avery. "The Metaphysics of Kantian Epistemology." *Proceedings of the American Catholic Philosophical Association* 76 (2002): 239–52. DOI: 10.5840/acpaproc2002762.

Greene, William Chase. "The Spirit of Comedy in Plato." *Harvard Studies in Classical Philology* 31 (1920): 63–123. DOI: 10.2307/310732

Hadot, Pierre. *Plotinus or The Simplicity of Vision*. Chicago: University of Chicago Press, 1993.

Hamington, Maurice. "A Father's Touch: Caring Embodiment and a Moral Revolution." In *Revealing Male Bodies*, 269–85. Bloomington: Indiana University Press, 2002.

Haraway, Donna J. *Staying with the Trouble: Making Kin in the Chthulucene*. Durham: Duke University Press Books, 2016.

Hegel, Georg Wilhelm Friedrich, Georg Lasson, and Eduard Gans. *Grundlinien der Philosophie des Rechts*. Leipzig: F. Meiner, 1911.

Heidegger, Martin. *Basic Writings from Being and Time (1927) to The Task of Thinking (1964)*. Vol. 2. San Francisco: Harper & Row, 1993.

———. "Der Ursprung des Kunstwerkes." In *Holzwege*, 1–74. Frankfurt am Main: Vittorio Klostermann, 1994.

———. *Die Technik und die Kehre*. Pfullingen: Verlag Günther Neske, 1991.

———. *Kant and the Problem of Metaphysics*. Translated by Richard Taft. Bloomington,: Indiana University Press, 1990.

———. "Kants These Über Das Sain." In *Wegmarken*, 445–80. Frankfurt am Main: Vittorio Klostermann, 1976.

———. *On Time and Being.* Translated by Joan Strambaugh. New York: Harper and Row, 1972.

———. *Poetry, Language, Thought.* Translated by Albert Hofstadter. New York: Harper and Row, 1971.

———. *The Question Concerning Technology, and Other Essays.* Translated by Willian Levitt. New York: Harper Torchbooks, 1977.

———. *Unterwegs zur Sprache.* Frankfurt am Main: Vittorio Klosterman, 1985.

Henrich, Dieter. "The Proof Structure of Kant's Transcendental Deduction." *Review of Metaphysics* 22, no. 4 (1969): 640–59. http://www.jstor.org/stable/20124942.

Hintikka, Jaakko. "Kant on Existence, Predication, and the Ontological Argument." In *The Logic of Being: Historical Studies,* 249–67. Dordrecht: D. Reidel, 1986.

Hölderlin, Friedrich. *Hymns and Fragments.* Translated by Richard Sieburth. Princeton: Princeton University Press, 1984.

Husserl, Edmund. *Die Krisis der europäischen Wissenschafen und die transzendentale Phänomenologie.* The Hague: Martinus Nijhoff, 1954.

Hyland, Drew A. *Finitude and Transcendence in the Platonic Dialogues.* Albany: State University of New York, 1995.

Jebb, Richard Claverhouse. *The Oedipus Tyrannus of Sophocles.* Cambridge: Cambridge University Press, 1963.

Jonas, Hans. "Plotin über Ewigkeit und Zeit." In *Politische Ordnung und menschliche Existenz: Festgabe für Eric Voegelin zum 60. Geburtstag,* 295–319. Munich: Verlag C.H. Beck, 1962.

———. "The Soul in Gnosticism and Plotinus." In *Philosophical Essays: From Ancient Creed to Technoligical Man,* 324–34. Chicago: The University of Chicago Press, 1974.

Kant, Immanuel. *Kant's Gesammelte Schriften (Akademie-Ausgabe).* Berlin: G. Reimer, 1902.

———. *Kritik der reinen Vernunft.* Hamburg: Meiner Verlag, 1990.

———. *Kritik der Urteilskraft*. Hamburg: Felix Meiner Verlag, 1990.

Kerínyi, Karl. "A Mythological Image of Girlhood." In *Facing the Gods,* edited by James Hillman, 39–45. Irving: Spring Publications, 1980.

Kristeva, Julia. *Powers of Horror: An Essay on Abjection.* Translated by Leon S. Roudiez. New York: Columbia University Press, 1982.

Laplanche, Jean, and J. B. Pontalis. *The Language of Psycho-Analysis.* 1st edition. New York: W.W. Norton, 1974.

Leroux, Georges. "Human Freedom in the Thought of Plotinus." In *The Cambridge Companion to Plotinus,* edited by Lloyd P. Gerson, 292–314. New York: Cambridge University Press, 1996.

Liddell, George Henry, and Robert Scott. *A Greek–English Lexicon*. Oxford: The Clarendon Press, 1968.

Lilly, Reginald. "The Topology of *Des Hégémonies brisées.*" *Research in Phenomenology* 28 (1998): 226–42. http://www.jstor.org/stable/24659058.

Long, Christopher P. *Aristotle on the Nature of Truth*. New York: Cambridge University Press, 2011.

———. "Care of Death: On the Teaching of Reiner Schürmann." *Philosophy Today,* January 31, 2017, 351–63. DOI: 10.5840/philtoday201713141.

———. "Dancing Naked with Socrates: Pericles, Aspasia and Socrates at Play with Politics, Rhetoric and Philosophy." *Ancient Philosophy* 23, no. 1 (2003): 49–69. DOI: 10.5840/ancientphil20032312

———. "Saving *Ta Legomena*: Aristotle and the History of Philosophy." *The Review of Metaphysics* 60, no. 2 (2006): 247–67. http://www.jstor.org/stable/20130776.

———. "The Daughters of Metis: Patriarchal Dominion and the Politics of the Between." *The Graduate Faculty Philosophy Journal* 28, no. 2 (2007): 67–86. DOI: 10.5840/gfpj20072824.

———. "The Duplicity of Beginning: Schürmann, Aristotle and the Origins of Metaphysics." *The Graduate Faculty*

Philosophy Journal 29, no. 2 (2008): 145–59. DOI: 10.5840/gfpj200829222.

———. *The Ethics of Ontology: Rethinking an Aristotelian Legacy.* Albany: State University of New York Press, 2004.

———. "The Voice of Singularity and a Philosophy to Come: Schürmann, Kant and the Pathology of Being." *Philosophy Today* 53, no. Supplement (2009): 138–50. DOI: 10.5840/philtoday200953Supplement37

———. "Two Powers, One Ability: The Understanding and Imagination in Kant's Critical Philosophy." *The Southern Journal of Philosophy* 36, no. 2 (1998): 233–53. DOI: 10.1111/j.2041-6962.1998.tb01754.x

——— and Richard A. Lee. "Between Reification and Mystification: Rethinking the Economy of Principles." *Telos* 120 (2001): 92–112. DOI: 10.17613/M6RW32

Lyotard, Jean-François. *The Differend: Phrases in Dispute.* Translated by Georges Van Den Abbeele. Minneapolis: University of Minnesota Press, 1988.

Manchester, Peter. "Time and the Soul in Plotinus, III 7 (45), 11." *Dionysius* 2 (1978): 101–36.

Merleau-Ponty, Maurice. *Phenomenology of Perception.* Translated by Colin Smith. 2nd edition. London and New York: Routledge, 2002.

———. *The Visible and the Invisible.* Edited by Claude Lefort. Translated by Alphonso Lingis. 1st edition. Northwestern University Press, 1968.

Mettes, Jeroen. "Political Poetry: A Few Notes. Poetics for N30." Translated by Vincent W.J. van Gerven Oei. *continent.* 2, no. 1 (2012). http://continentcontinent.cc/index.php/continent/article/view/80.

Moore, Christopher. *Socrates and Self-Knowledge.* First edition. Cambridge: Cambridge University Press, 2015.

Narbonne, Jean-Marc. *La Métaphysique de Plotin.* Paris: Librairie Philosophique J. Vrin, 1994.

Owens, Joseph. *The Doctrine of Being in the Aristotelian Metaphysics.* Toronto: Pontifical Institute of Mediaeval Studies, 1978.

Piore, Nancy Kline. *Lightning: The Poetry of René Char.* Boston: Northeastern University Press, 1981.

Plato. *Platonis Opera.* Vols. I–V. New York: Oxford University Press, 1995.

Plotinus. *The Enneads.* Translated by Stephen MacKenna. London: Penguin Books, 1991.

———, A.H. Armstrong, and Porphyry. *Plotinus.* Cambridge: Harvard University Press, 1966.

Rist, John M. *Plotinus: The Road to Reality.* Cambridge: Cambridge University Press, 1967.

Sachs, Joe. *Aristotle: Nicomachean Ethics.* Newburyport: Focus Publishing, 2002.

Schürmann, Reiner. *Broken Hegemonies.* Translated by Reginald Lilly. Bloomington: Indiana University Press, 2003.

———. "Conditions of Evil." In *Deconstruction and the Possibility of Justice,* edited by Drucilla Cornell, Michel Rosenfeld, and David Gray Carlson, 387–403. New York: Routledge, 1992.

———. "Abstraction That Makes the Viewer Think About the Last Paintings of Louis Comtois." *C Magazine,* no. 29 (1991): 6–7.

———. *Heidegger on Being and Acting: From Principles to Anarchy.* Bloomington: Indiana University Press, 1987.

———. "Le praxis symbolique." *Cahiers Internationaux de Symbolisme* 29–30 (1976): 145–70.

———. "Legislation-Transgression: Strategies and Counter-Strategies in the Transcendental Justification of Norms." *Man and World* 17 (1984): 361–98.

———. "Situating René Char: Hölderlin, Heidegger, Char and the 'There Is.'" *boundary 2* 4, no. 2 (January 1, 1976): 513–34. doi:10.2307/302151.

———. "Symbolic Difference." *The Graduate Faculty Philosophy Journal* 19/20, no. 2/1 (1997): 9–38. DOI: 10.5840/gfpj199719/202/12.

———. "Symbolic Praxis." *The Graduate Faculty Philosophy Journal* 19/20, no. 2/1 (1997): 39–65. DOI: 10.5840/gfpj199719/202/14.

Smith, Andrew. "Review: Tolma in Plotinus." *The Classical Review* 46, no. 1 (1996): 76–78. DOI: 10.1093/cr/46.1.76.

Smyth, Herbert Weir. *Greek Grammar.* Cambridge: Harvard University Press, 1956.

Sommerstein, Alan H. *Aeschylus: Eumenides.* Cambridge: Cambridge University Press, 1989.

Sophocles. *Antigone.* Edited by Mark Griffith. Cambridge University Press, 1999.

———. *Sophoclis Fabulae.* Oxford: Clarendon Press, 1990.

———. *The Theban Plays.* Translated by Ruby Blondell. Newburyport: Focus Publishing, 2004.

Thucydides. *Historiae I.* Oxford: Oxford University Press, 1942.

Torchia, N. Joseph. *Plotinus, Tolma, and the Descent of Being: An Exposition and Analysis.* New York: P. Lang, 1993.

Tyrrell, William Blake, and Larry J. Bennett. "Pericles' Muting of Women's Voices in Thuc. 2.45.2." *The Classical Journal* 95, no. 1 (1999): 37–51. http://www.jstor.org/stable/3298233.

Winnington-Ingram, R. P. "A Religious Function of Greek Tragedy: A Study in the Oedipus Coloneus and the Oresteia." *The Journal of Hellenic Studies* 74 (1954): 16–24. DOI: 10.2307/627550.

Wollheim, Richard. *Sigmund Freud.* New York: Viking Press, 1971.

*

"W. dreams, like Phaedrus, of an army of thinker-friends, thinker-lovers. He dreams of a thought-army, a thought-pack, which would storm the philosophical Houses of Parliament. He dreams of Tartars from the philosophical steppes, of thought-barbarians, thought-outsiders. What distance would shine in their eyes!"

— Lars Iyer

www.ingramcontent.com/pod-product-compliance
Lightning Source LLC
Chambersburg PA
CBHW072046160426
43197CB00014B/2647